Life

according to

JESUS

WISDOM FOR LIVING EACH DAY TO THE FULLEST

Jack Graham

Tyndale House Publishers, Inc.
WHEATON, ILLINOIS

To my lifelong friend, Dr. O.S. Hawkins, whose life and ministry have intersected with mine through the years. I express profound gratitude for your faithful life, inspiring faith, and encouraging love.

Visit Tyndale's exciting Web site at www.tyndale.com

Copyright © 2004 by Jack Graham. All rights reserved.

Cover author photo courtesy of C. David Edmonson

Barbara Kois collaborated in writing this book.

Designed by Timothy R. Botts

Library of Congress Cataloging-in-Publication Data

Graham, Jack, date.
  Life according to Jesus : wisdom for living each day to the fullest / Jack Graham.
    p. cm.
  ISBN 0-8423-7466-3 (pbk.)
  1, Bible. N.T. John—Devotional literature. I. Title.
BS2615.54.G73 2004
242'.5—dc22   2003024808

Printed in the United States of America.

09 08 07 06 05 04
 8   7   6   5   4   3   2   1

Table of Contents

ACKNOWLEDGMENTS

For the wonderful and dynamic people of Prestonwood Baptist Church whose love for Christ and God's Word inspire their grateful pastor every day.

The staff of Prestonwood for your excellence in ministry and dedication to the work of the church. And to the PowerPoint radio and television team which delivers the message of Life across America.

For the sixteen million Southern Baptists who have given me the privilege of serving as their President. I am extremely grateful for my Baptist legacy and the continued influence of over forty thousand Southern Baptist churches in fulfilling the Great Commission around the world.

To Barbara Kois whose expertise and editing enabled my words and messages to reach the larger audience of this book.

Thank you.

FOREWORD
JOSH McDOWELL

Having spent most of my life amazed by the evidence for Jesus Christ, I have documented hard evidence that shows that he is the Son of God who loved us and gave his life for our sins to reconcile us to God. However, some of the greatest evidence comes in the form of changed lives: desperate lives that now have hope, fearful lives that now know peace, and empty lives that are now full to overflowing.

The book of John presents a number of these dramatically changed lives. Jack Graham, my pastor and my friend, brings these people to life for us and shows how we can access the same awesome power that changed their lives.

As I sit under the teaching of Dr. Graham, I continually gain new insights. His understanding of both the Bible and the human condition, combined with his knowledge of people based on years of experience as a pastor, allow him to illumine God's Word in fresh ways week after week.

And now Jack has gone one step further in this book. He has taken the teaching material from his popular sermon series on the book of John and applied his lessons and insights to the tough issues people face today. He doesn't hesitate to tackle challenging topics like freedom from addiction, religious snobbery, and the insidious attraction of false gods in today's culture. He uses real talk for the real problems of today. He shows us a strong and passionate Jesus who is tender, compassionate, and very real himself—the God-man who doesn't shy away from controversy.

As one examines statistics about signs of decay in our society, like the use of illegal drugs, teen suicide, and a pervading sense of despair, you know that we need a complete turnaround from where we are today. We need a revolution that will replace status quo thinking with transformed minds and lives. And that is only possible when people come face-to-face with Jesus, the One we find spotlighted in this book.

So get ready for a change because this book will transform the way you see Jesus and also the way you live your life.

SECTION **I**

Maker of My Life

LIGHT FOR THE PATH

 Life itself was in him, and this life gives light to everyone. The light shines through the darkness, and the darkness can never extinguish it. John 1:4-5

A MOM AND DAD with three preschool children were part of a group hiking through the woods at twilight, observing the habitat of nocturnal creatures who only venture out at dark. One of the little boys wanted to climb up on a log at the side of the pathway and jump off, so the family paused while he did so. Naturally, the other two children had to climb up and jump off as well, and during the process the other hikers got far enough ahead that the family could no longer see where they were or in which direction they had gone.

In the deepening darkness, the parents didn't want to alarm the children by shouting for the group or calling for help, so they began to sing hymns, hoping they would be heard and rescued. Sure enough, a welcome flashlight shone in their direction a few minutes into the second song, and they escaped a night of sleeping in the damp marsh and eating bugs for dinner.

When we cry out to God, whether we sing hymns, sob in grief, or talk to Him in the quietness of our room, He hears. He is eager to shine His light on our path and bring us back into His group, the church, the body of Christ. Having created us for a relationship with Him, His ears are always turned toward those who love Him.

What does John's description mean to us living in this third millennium? John talked about two of Jesus' roles in these verses: He is the Creator-God and He is the source of life and light. Understanding these roles can deepen our appreciation of His authenticity. His creativity made the world, His light illumines it, and His superintendence allows it to function.

Whatever people may think causes the world to go around, the true power is Jesus Christ. Without Him, nothing exists.

First, Jesus is the Creator-God. As God, He is sovereign, the supreme ruler of the entire universe. Matthew emphasized Jesus' sovereignty in his Gospel which is the most "Jewish" of the four books. From his perspective, proving that Jesus of Nazareth was the promised Messiah of the Old Testament was paramount. So he portrayed Christ as a sovereign, the king of Israel. Matthew was right to present Jesus as sovereign. Though humans resist the idea of anyone ruling over us, that is what a sovereign does. From the Old Testament (Zechariah 8:23) to the New (Philippians 2:10), Scripture tells us that Christ is King over all.

The great news is that nothing of ours is too hard for the Sovereign Ruler of the universe. Not job difficulties, wayward children, or sick family members. Because He is sovereign, He knows what lies ahead on our life path when we can't see farther than the present, so He can light the way for us.

Since He made us, He thoroughly knows how we "work." He knows how to get our attention, how to lavish abundant gifts on us and give us our hearts' desires, and how to slowly but surely grow us into people who act and talk and live and love like Jesus. It takes a lifetime of growth, but our Creator is very patient.

Second, Jesus is the true source of life and light. He made us, gave us life, and promised to guide us in the way we should go. "Trust in the LORD with all your heart; do not depend on your own understanding. Seek his will in all you do, and he will direct your paths" (Proverbs 3:5-6). We can count on His promise to light our way if we but ask Him.

What about You? Next time you are lost and can't find your way or life's pressures seem too much to handle, turn to your Creator, your source of life. He is the ever present light waiting to take your hand and lead you along your life path. Do you honestly believe He's able? Check Him out. As you lean heavily on God, you'll find Him trustworthy.

Take a Look As you read Isaiah 40:12-27, write down ten examples of God's complete sovereignty, or control over the world and everything in it. As Isaiah asks in verse 18, "To whom, then, can we compare God?"

TRUE OR FALSE

 But although the world was made through him, the world didn't recognize him when he came. Even in his own land and among his own people, he was not accepted. But to all who believed him and accepted him, he gave the right to become children of God. John 1:10-12

MANY PEOPLE talk about God, but which "god" do they mean? Even during His days on earth, the world didn't recognize Jesus as God, and that confusion still exists today. Many believe that Jesus was simply a great man or a respected prophet. Others believe that all roads lead to heaven, whether we follow Jesus, Muhammad, or Buddha. Without knowing who Jesus really is—the Son of God and the only Savior—we may try to fill our inner longing with false gods such as money, success, or even harmful behaviors. We may try to please God with good works or even self-sacrifice, rather than receiving the free gift of salvation Jesus offers.

While the God of the Bible is a loving God, the many deities of mythology were capricious, jealous, and petty. Since they were created by people, they reflected all the weaknesses of mankind. The true and living God, on the other hand, has none of our faults. Instead, He has created us in His image, imparting many of His characteristics to us. He is trustworthy, steadfast, and certain.

Even as Christians, we still sometimes create petty gods without realizing it. We may idolize our accomplishments, our pleasures, other people, or material things. We might deny our idolatry because we don't "worship" these things, in the sense of giving religious reverence to them, as the dictionary describes the word. Think about the following questions: Are your thoughts focused continually on one part of your life, almost to the exclusion of others? Do you habitually and almost compulsively perform particular behaviors again and again? Are you devoted to a person or the pursuit of a particular goal at the expense of other areas of life? If you answered yes to any of these questions, you may be worshiping a false god, one that will surely disappoint.

Think of the man who travels so extensively as he climbs the ladder of success that he misses out on his children's growing-up years, or the woman who strives to please her unpleasable husband until he leaves her for another woman. Their gods have let them down, as false gods always will.

But Jesus will always do what is best for you. He has promised to bring good out of even the most horrible circumstances, and He does that time and again.

Rachel Scott was one of the high school students killed in the Columbine High School tragedy in 1999. She was killed because she was a Christian who was not afraid to talk about her love for Jesus. While her parents, friends, and teachers were heartbroken because of her death and the deaths of the others in the incident, God brought good out of the evil of that unforgettable day. After her death, other students gave their lives to God as a result of her courage and faith.

But false gods are just the opposite of the one true God. While He brings good out of evil, false gods insert evil into good things. For example, eating is a natural and necessary physical function, and delicious food is another of God's gifts. But food, misused and over—or under—eaten, becomes an idol when it becomes one's focus and ruins lives with obesity or anorexia.

Three key characteristics distinguish Jesus from the false gods. First, He is equal with God the Father and God the Spirit. This has been the belief of the Christian church since the beginning. In A.D. 325 this belief was formalized in a Trinitarian creed (the Nicene Creed) to counter a heresy that was attempting to demote Christ from His place as equal with God. And that heresy is still around today.

If you haven't already experienced it, one day you will answer your door and find yourself face-to-face with members of a religious cult who claim to be Christians—but they aren't. They don't believe Jesus was God. They will say He was "a" god but not "the" God. Those who assert that Jesus did not preexist his earthly life nor create the world rob Jesus of His equal and eternal place with God.

Second, Jesus is essentially God. God is three-in-one, a trinity of beings. They are not different manifestations of one being. Some people believe God morphed Himself into a human being and came to earth as Jesus. Another misbelief is that the Holy Spirit isn't really a person, just the power of God being unleashed. The Father, Son, and Spirit are all distinct persons— and all God (Philippians 2:5-11).

Third, Jesus is eternally God. Another thing the Nicene Creed states with certainty is the biblical doctrine that Jesus was "begotten, not made." That is, He wasn't created. He is, and always has been, infinite and eternal. A Jesus who isn't eternal Himself could hardly provide eternal life for you.

Like Paul, we need to "know whom [we] have believed" (2 Timothy 1:12 NKJV) and, with Peter, why we believe (1 Peter 3:15). We need to know how to tell a false god from the real God, because the difference is a matter of life and death, a choice between a fruitful, productive life and a tormented life, between freedom and bondage.

What about You? What are the gods in your life? Be honest. Who or what occupies the majority of your thought life? Are there behaviors or habits that you do repeatedly and know you should stop? The real God, Jesus Christ, will help you to dethrone the false god as you turn again and again to the One who is true.

Take a Look Read the creation story in Genesis 1. What did God start with and what did He end up with on day six of Creation?

RELIGIOUS SNOBBERY

 There was a man of the Pharisees named Nicodemus, a ruler of the Jews. This man came to Jesus by night and said to Him, "Rabbi, we know that You are a teacher come from God; for no one can do these signs that You do unless God is with him."
John 3:1-2 NKJV

NICODEMUS HAD a problem many people have today. He felt spiritually superior to others. He was religious, he was respected, and he kept all the rules.

Some Christians today also believe that since they obey the rules, go to church, and give their money, they're above those who don't. They may even secretly wonder whether their success in life doesn't somehow reflect God's pleasure in how they live, as in "I do what I'm supposed to do, and God has rewarded me for that."

But in Luke 18:11-13, Jesus dashed that way of thinking when He told the parable of the Pharisee and the tax collector. Jesus cut to the heart of the matter when He said the proud Pharisee thanked God that he was not a sinner like everyone else, especially the tax collector. All the hated tax collector could say to God was, "Be merciful to me, for I am a sinner." Jesus' point was that the proud will be humbled and the humble will be honored. Jesus is so good at standing human wisdom on its head. The honored fellow would be brought low and the despised man would be forgiven.

We don't really know why Nicodemus approached Jesus at night, although we know he was intellectually interested in the miracles Jesus had done. Perhaps he was afraid of what his religious cohorts would say or was ashamed to be seen talking to a lowly carpenter. Or he might have had spiritual questions that could not wait until the next day—questions about Jesus being the long-awaited Messiah.

Men in Nicodemus's part of the world engaged in their deepest conversations in the evening when the time for work was over. They gathered to talk about philosophy or spiritual matters. Perhaps he came at night for a long and interesting talk. He addressed Jesus formally, as *Rabbi*. He was self-sufficient, confident, and curious, but he didn't know the true need of his heart and life—his need for Jesus.

To Jesus, Nicodemus's position as an educated Pharisee meant nothing. Some of His most scathing rebukes were directed at the religious leaders and their pompous hypocrisy. Most of the time, He chose to be with those who were rejected by society—the unsophisticated, plain, authentic people who truly understood their need for Jesus.

Think of Zacchaeus, the scorned man who stole some of his people's taxes for himself. Yet Jesus loved him and called him to come down out of the tree, singling him out and visiting his house. Or the woman at the well, who was spurned because of her marital history. Or Mary Magdalene, a prostitute. Jesus seemed to specialize in befriending outcasts, and there are many examples of that in the Bible.

Jesus chooses authentic people to spend time with.

What about You? Are you drawn to those rejected by most people? Do you tend to approach people whose needs are most obvious? Or are you attracted to success and beauty and repelled by failure?

Jesus loved the outcasts, and He never hesitated to put the arrogant religious leaders in their places. How can you make your church and your home places where those with the greatest needs will experience the love of Christ when they enter? He singled them out for attention; we can do it too.

Take a Look Read James 2:2-5 and write a sentence explaining how we should treat people. How should a shabbily dressed person be greeted in church? And what about the elegantly dressed person? What, indeed, would Jesus do?

STARTING OVER

 Jesus answered and said to him, "Most assuredly, I say to you, unless one is born again, he cannot see the kingdom of God." Nicodemus said to Him, "How can a man be born when he is old? Can he enter a second time into his mother's womb and be born?" Jesus answered, "Most assuredly, I say to you, unless one is born of water and the Spirit, he cannot enter the kingdom of God." John 3:3-5 NKJV

THE MIRACLE OF BIRTH. A parent who sees his or her new-born child emerge into the world is often awestruck. The physical act of giving birth is astonishing; the way the human body works to produce a new life is almost beyond understanding. New parents often can't take their eyes off that tiny person given to them to love and care for.

Years ago, an Oklahoma doctor delivered a baby after the mother struggled for hours even though her own life was in danger. When someone described the birth as a miracle, the doctor said, "Every birth is a miracle."

But as amazing as the physical process of birth is, it can happen only once. There's no going back from whence we came. Imagine Nicodemus's surprise and the mental pictures his mind must have conjured when Jesus told him he needed to be born again.

His rhetorical question as to how a man can be born when he is old probably meant something like, "I'm an old man now and I can't start over." He had devoted himself to religion. He was willing to study the law of the Jews, to obey its many commandments as well as the traditions of the religious leaders. He even taught the law to others. But he was incredulous at the thought of a new birth.

Jesus told him he could do it. He could start over because it's never too late. Stubborn hearts can be softened. Attitudes can change and lifelong patterns can be broken. True change can occur.

What did Nicodemus need to do? The same thing each of us needs to do—tell Jesus that we need Him and we want to be born again, to experience the authentic miracle only He can do, the miracle of new birth. Have you done that? Have you told Him you have sinned and asked Him to forgive you? Have you asked Him to handle your life from now on and be your Savior? The Bible promises that by doing that, you, too, can be born again. "For whoever calls on the name of the Lord shall be saved" (Romans 10:13 NKJV).

What about You? Do you think you're too old to start again, too set in your ways and habits? Jesus says it's never too late for a new birth when you place your life in His hands, or for a renewal of your heart when you give Him additional parts of your life to handle. It wasn't too late for Nicodemus, and it isn't too late for you.

Take a Look Second Corinthians 5:17 says, "What this means is that those who become Christians become new persons. They are not the same anymore, for the old life is gone. A new life has begun!" Read to the end of 2 Corinthians chapter 5, noting the purpose for which we have new life in Christ.

MIRACLES WITH A MESSAGE

 But I have a greater witness than John's; for the works which the Father has given Me to finish—the very works that I do— bear witness of Me, that the Father has sent Me.
John 5:36 NKJV

MAGICIAN HARRY HOUDINI was famous for his ability to free himself from handcuffs, chains, and ropes. Houdini began life as Ehrich Weiss in 1874 in Budapest, Hungary. His family was poor, and at age eight Ehrich sold newspapers and polished boots to earn money. When his father took him to a magic show, Ehrich was entranced, and his first performance as a magician took place when he was just nine. At fifteen, he read an autobiography of French magician Jean Robert-Houdin, and decided to change his name to Houdini, adding the letter "i," which means "like." He performed twenty shows a day, earning just twelve dollars a week.

Interestingly, Houdini spent much of his life debunking the supposed powers of spiritualists and mediums. He knew they were fakes and that his own abilities came from sleight of hand, physical agility, and much practice.

Houdini never claimed that his feats were miracles, but Jesus' works were very different. There was no human explanation for what He was able to do; no sleight of hand or fancy footwork could accomplish those feats. And with every one of Jesus' miracles, there was a message.

To the couple who had run out of wine at their wedding in Cana, He showed that He is the answer for life's disappointments. To the nobleman with the sick son, Jesus showed He was the answer for doubt, and the man believed. For the paralyzed man, Jesus demonstrated that He is God's answer for disabilities and frailties. When He fed the five thousand, He showed that He is the answer for our needs and desires. When He walked on the water, He demonstrated that He is the answer for life's dark times and storms. When He healed the blind man, He showed that He has the answer even when we can't see it. And when He raised Lazarus from the dead, He showed He is God's answer for death.

The miracles Jesus performed were also evidence as to who He is. They identified Him as God, able to do great works. In Luke 5:23-26, Jesus said:

> "Is it easier to say, 'Your sins are forgiven' or 'Get up and walk'? I will prove that I, the Son of Man, have the authority on earth to forgive sins." Then Jesus turned to the paralyzed man and said, "Stand up, take your mat, and go on home, because you are healed!" And immediately, as everyone watched, the man jumped to his feet, picked up his mat, and went home praising God. Everyone was gripped with great wonder and awe. And they praised God, saying over and over again, "We have seen amazing things today."

Recall that Nicodemus said in John 3:2 (NKJV), "we know that You are a teacher come from God; for no one can do these signs that You do unless God is with him."

Some people argue that the miracles in the Bible aren't true because it's difficult to believe in supernatural events. They say we need to take the miracles out of the Bible so we can more easily believe it and see Christ who spoke wonderful words, and who came as a social outcast and overturned society. But if you remove the miracles, you strip Jesus of His deity. He was and is God, who controls time and history, who is able to do what God and God alone can do. Jesus said these miracles, signs, and wonders tell us who He is. They prove His veracity.

If the Bible were stripped of the miracles, we would miss the message, the central theme; we would miss discovering the reality of God in Jesus Christ.

Jesus' miracles were not tricks or publicity stunts; they had a purpose. Houdini's purpose was to amaze people by his physical abilities, nothing more. Jesus' purpose was to show the people then and us today that He is the only answer to our every need and situation.

What about You? Which of the specific needs Jesus met in the miracles are you experiencing today? Is it disappointment like the wedding couple? Or doubt like the centurion with the sick son? Or disability and frailty like the paralyzed man? Or the despair and darkness of a storm? Or are you even facing death? Will you believe that Jesus is the answer to your need and that He will provide for you as He did for all of these people?

Take a Look Read Matthew 8:14-17. What additional purpose did Jesus' miracles accomplish?

AN UNSINKABLE PLAN

 They were three or four miles out when suddenly they saw Jesus walking on the water toward the boat. They were terrified, but he called out to them, "I am here! Don't be afraid." Then they were eager to let him in, and immediately the boat arrived at their destination! John 6:19-21

ONE OF MY FAVORITE places in the Holy Land is the Sea of Galilee. A sunrise or sunset reflecting on the surface of this large lake creates a picture of serenity. But a storm that can suddenly rage across its surface changes the picture to one of severity. Screaming down from the high mountains surrounding the Sea of Galilee, the winds quickly transform the lake from a place of calm beauty to one of fear.

The disciples, some of whom were professional fishermen, knew both scenarios well. But when they set out across the lake in their boat, they were fresh from the miracle of the loaves and fishes, confident in Jesus' ability and desire to care for them. The upbeat atmosphere in the boat was one of joy and celebration.

They were about to learn that whether times are good or bad, Jesus has a plan. In Matthew's version of the story (Matthew 14:22), "Jesus made his disciples get back into the boat and cross to the other side of the lake while he sent the people home." He sent them out onto a peaceful lake that was about to turn quickly into a tempest. They were caught in the storm— without Him.

Imagine their fear, the fear of perishing on an angry sea. Fear is a real part of our lives, too, because we live in a dangerous world. Media stories bombard us with violence and tragedy, and many people today are more concerned with their personal safety and security than ever before.

The disciples' fear was intensely personal, as this storm could mean life or death for them. They faced a physical storm, and like the various kinds of storms we face in life, it was scary. Like these men, we also worry about the outcome; we wonder if we will survive.

Is it possible to get to a calm place in the midst of the storm? The disciples found that indeed it is. The first crucial step is to realize that God has a plan. Just as Jesus sent the disciples to the boat, He has directed your path to where you are today. Of course, your choices have made a difference, but even they are not beyond His ability to use for good. He knew the storm was coming, but He sent them out in the boat anyway. The squall struck suddenly, like squalls often do in our lives: The phone rings, the doctor's report comes in, your supervisor tells you your employment is over.

Even in the face of problems, God is still sovereign; He is still in control. He allows storms to teach us, to increase our faith, and to grow our character. The disciples, in the middle of the storm, were separated from Jesus, or so they thought. Sometimes in the middle of a crisis it feels like God is a million miles away. We can't see Him, we can't feel His presence, and we cry out to Him to come help us. When He delays, we wonder why. The disciples must have also wondered why He let them go out into this storm. And then they saw Him. He had a real plan to save them, just as He has a real and specific plan for each of us.

What about You? Perhaps your fears aren't about problems out there in the larger world, but rather they are personal fears, close-up fears that you face alone. It may be the fear of disease, or of losing your mate or your job, or of something bad happening to your children. What is your own personal fear? What haunts your heart?

As much as we shun difficulty, problems, and heartaches, some of our richest growth comes from those hard times. Afterward, we often see His hand and His plan, a plan for good and not for evil (Jeremiah 29:11). Just as the disciples were not really alone in the boat, neither are we. Jesus is there, a still spot in the middle of the storm, ready and willing to calm our fears.

Take a Look Second Timothy 1:7 (NKJV) assures us that "God has not given us a spirit of fear, but of power and of love and of a sound mind."

Look up this verse in another version of the Bible and compare the words. Make a list of what God is promising us in this verse.

ACTIONS SPEAK LOUDER

 So Jesus told them, "I'm not teaching my own ideas, but those of God who sent me. Anyone who wants to do the will of God will know whether my teaching is from God or is merely my own. Those who present their own ideas are looking for praise for themselves, but those who seek to honor the one who sent them are good and genuine." John 7:16-18

THE JEWISH LEADERS couldn't figure Him out. They asked, "Is He a good man? Or a deceiver? How does He know so much when He hasn't studied as we have? Maybe He has a demon. . . ."

They didn't understand Him, partly because they were blinded by their own sense of superiority and partly because they hadn't spent much time with Him, listening and watching. When they did listen to Him, it was with a suspicious, critical ear, hoping to catch Him in an error. They could have studied His words in light of the Scriptures they already possessed, concluding that He was teaching God's ideas and that He represented God here on earth. But they chose not to.

One of the best ways to get to know someone is to examine his message and see if it lines up with his actions. Someone once said, "If a person shows you who he is, believe him." In other words, if his actions conflict with his words, realize that the actions are probably more indicative of the real person behind the words.

If a friend claims to love you but criticizes you to others and passes along confidential information you've asked her not to share, the word "love" is not backed up by her actions, and you may begin to conclude that she is not the close friend she claims to be.

Jesus' words always lined up with His actions because His words were those of the One who sent Him, God the Father. He was deeply acquainted with His Father, and He was able to speak and act in ways consistent with God's ideas.

Jesus spoke of forgiveness, and He also forgave. In Mark 2:5, when four friends lowered the paralyzed man down through the roof, Jesus said, "My son, your sins are forgiven." When the broken woman came to Jesus in Luke 7, her tears landed on His feet and she wiped His feet with her hair. He said, in verse 48, "Your sins are forgiven."

He spoke of compassion, and He showed compassion. In Matthew 14:14 and elsewhere He showed compassion by healing the sick in the crowd. He spoke of obedience, and He obeyed His Father, even by dying on the cross (Philippians 2:8). Jesus' words and actions were those of God; His actions were consistent with what He said.

The best way to discern truth from a lie is whether it agrees with the Bible. Does it conflict with something the Bible says? Does it contradict the Bible? If so, it's not true, nor is it from God. When a murderer says, "God told me to kill those people," we immediately know he was deceived because God condemns murder. If a married woman says, "I believe God brought this man into my life because my husband just doesn't listen to me," she's deceiving herself. God never brings adulterous relationships into our lives.

What about You? How do you handle messages or information that doesn't sound quite right to you? What standard do you measure it against?

The message of Jesus never contradicts the Scriptures. He has shown us who He is and what He expects of us. We need to use the Bible as the ultimate authority for all truth.

Take a Look Second John 1:4-11 delineates the difference between true and false teaching. Find at least one distinguishing mark of each that believers are to constantly watch out for.

THE LIFE EVERYBODY WANTS

 I have come that they may have life, and that they may have it more abundantly. John 10:10 NKJV

LONGER LIFE. Optimism. Faster healing. Is this the beginning of a vitamin advertisement or a promotion for an herbal diet supplement that will do everything except cover gray hair?

No, it's a description of the life of faith. Studies have shown that people of faith live longer, healthier lives. People who pray and are prayed for get well faster and more often.

Recent research has shown that church attendance helps even sick people feel more optimistic and hopeful, and immune function is enhanced by feelings of togetherness and social interaction.

Of course, that doesn't mean believers never get sick or die, but it shows that what the Bible says about the many benefits of a relationship with God is true. In Proverbs, we see the following: "Let your heart keep my commands; for length of days and long life and peace they will add to you" (Proverbs 3:1-2 NKJV). And in Proverbs 3:16 (NKJV) God promises, "Length of days is in [wisdom's] right hand, in her left hand riches and honor."

Many people mistakenly believe that God is angry with them and wants to punish them, but the Bible is full of colorful descriptions of the richness of a life lived close to God. While He is angry at sin and evil, He loves His children very much. In that love, He has provided a way of forgiveness and restoration of our relationship with Him in Jesus Christ.

Jesus came into a poverty-stricken world, a world steeped in the darkness of sin. And He came with the most extravagant gift ever given, the gift of His life so that we could have real and vibrant life in living color.

The word used for *abundant* in John 10:10 is a word that describes the rising of the waves on the ocean. If you sit and watch the waves, you'll see that they just keep coming; they never stop. That's the description of what it means to know Christ—wave after wave of His pure and genuine love, grace, and power in our lives. The waves rise and overflow the shore with the fullness of life God gives.

The abundant life is fresh, not stale. It is straightforward, honest, and clean. Just as the waves wash away all the footprints on the sand and leave the beach fresh and unmarked, our lives are fresh and new each day as we live for Christ and turn away from sin. The abundant life is a life of freedom; we don't have to stay in our old habits and sinful patterns. Jesus provides the power to say no. And the abundant life is a fruitful life, a life that reproduces itself in the lives of others. It is involvement in an effort beyond oneself. It recognizes that life is God's gift to us. The way we use our lives is how we can give a gift back to God.

What about You? Are you living a full, abundant life? Not necessarily a busy life or a hectic life, but a life full of people and productivity and purpose? Or do you feel empty, burned out, and used up?

It's not the length of your life; it's the depth of your life that matters. It's not a trouble-free life; it's what you do with the problems and how you respond to challenge and difficulty that counts.

Abundant life is available to you because Jesus wants to add life and vitality to your years. Give Him your days, weeks, months, and years. Give Him all of your life and ask Him to make it an abundant, overflowing, generous life. He wants to do that for you and He will.

Take a Look Find one characteristic of the abundant life promised in Isaiah 26:3. Find three characteristics someone with an abundant life should exhibit as described in Romans 12:10.

LIFE OR DEATH

 Jesus said to her, "I am the resurrection and the life. He who believes in Me, though he may die, he shall live. And whoever lives and believes in Me shall never die. Do you believe this?"
John 11:25-26 NKJV

AFTER HIS INVOLVEMENT in approximately 130 deaths by physician-assisted suicide or euthanasia, Jack Kevorkian, "Doctor Death," finally went to jail in 1999. He was convicted of first-degree murder in the death of Thomas Youk, a fifty-two-year-old man who suffered from Lou Gehrig's disease. Another Kevorkian victim, fifty-eight-year-old Marjorie Wantz had been diagnosed as depressed and suicidal by psychiatrists who believed her pelvic pain to be psychosomatic. After her death, an autopsy found no physical cause for her pain, and yet Kevorkian helped her die anyway. In another case in 1993, seventy-year-old Hugh Gale, who had emphysema and congestive heart disease, allegedly changed his mind at the last minute, but Kevorkian didn't stop the death process and Gale died.

In total violation of the oath doctors take to preserve life, Kevorkian invented a "death machine" in 1989 for people to use in committing suicide. He built the device from thirty dollars' worth of scrap parts purchased at garage sales and hardware stores.

What a contrast between the doctor of death and Jesus who brings life. Kevorkian turned living people into dead ones; Jesus brought the dead to life.

In John 11, Jesus' friend Lazarus became very sick. His sisters, Mary and Martha, sent word to Jesus that their brother was desperately ill. Imagine their disappointment when Jesus didn't come and Lazarus died.

It wasn't that Jesus couldn't get there in time to save Lazarus or that He didn't know how sick he was. Jesus had a better plan in mind, a plan to prove the power of God.

When He finally arrived, both women spoke of their faith and their disappointment. Martha said, "Lord, if You had been here, my brother would not have died. But even now I know that whatever You ask of God, God will give You" (John 11:21-22 NKJV) and Mary said almost the same thing in verse 32. They didn't get angry at Him; they didn't ask, "Why us?" They simply expressed their sorrow and their belief that He could have kept their brother alive.

Jesus' heartfelt compassion prevailed, as always, and He raised Lazarus from the dead. He brought life from death, joy from sadness, celebration from grief.

Sometimes when we're in the throes of pain or loss, it's tempting to despair of life, to forget that Jesus is the answer to life's tragedies, that He will one day wipe away every tear and right every wrong. We may feel like giving up, like there's no point in continuing to try to keep going, to keep plodding along through the swamps of illness or loss.

But like these sisters, we, too, can take our pain to Jesus and find Him deeply compassionate.

What about You?   Have there been times in your life when you felt as if the pain was just too much for you to keep on living? Are you there right now, wondering if life is really worth living?

God never wastes our pain, as agonizing as it can be. He promises to work good in your life even from the worst circumstances—maybe not today or tomorrow, but eventually.

Take your pain, your despair, your hopelessness to Jesus. As He wept for Lazarus, He weeps for your suffering as well. As He called Lazarus, He will also call your name and say, "Come forth. Come forth from your pain and despair into the comfort that only I can give."

Take a Look   Isaiah predicted Jesus' suffering in Isaiah 53. As you read this chapter, find at least five ways Jesus suffered.

GOING DOWN TO GET UP

 Most assuredly, I say to you, unless a grain of wheat falls into the ground and dies, it remains alone; but if it dies, it produces much grain. He who loves his life will lose it, and he who hates his life in this world will keep it for eternal life. If anyone serves Me, let him follow Me; and where I am, there My servant will be also. If anyone serves Me, him My Father will honor. John 12:24-26 NKJV

PAM ARRANGED her seed packets on the kitchen table. Marigolds, zinnias, nasturtiums, and tomatoes. *What am I forgetting? I know I bought another vegetable,* she thought. She rifled through her kitchen drawer where she usually kept her seeds, saw no additional packets, and went to her porch "greenhouse" to place the tiny seeds in lumps of soil in divided containers. She watered the planted seeds gently and covered them with plastic lids, eager for germination to occur so she could see the results of her efforts.

Four weeks later it was time to transplant the seedlings outdoors, and after additional weeks of fertilizing, watering, and weeding her garden, Pam had a crop of flowers and tomatoes. As she got out her large wooden salad bowl, she remembered what she had forgotten to plant, and she again searched her seed drawer. Underneath stamps and envelopes and other assorted papers was a packet of romaine lettuce seeds, unplanted and unsprouted. *I'll have to buy lettuce this year because it's too late for these,* she thought. Seeds can't produce crops unless they are planted.

In John 12:24-26 Jesus spoke of His death on the cross which produced salvation for all who believe. Our salvation couldn't have happened unless He died, really died. Some have said He merely swooned or slept, but His death was real, and His death brought life in one of the many paradoxes in the Bible.

In Matthew 5:4 (NKJV), Jesus said, "Blessed are those who mourn."And in 2 Corinthians 12:10, Paul said, "When I am weak, then I am strong." Jesus said if you want to live, then die. He didn't say whoever makes it to chairman or whoever can climb to the CEO position or earn a million dollars will be great in heaven—just the opposite. Those things won't count at all, but what was done with humility and genuine service will last. After all, He came as a servant, "Just as the Son of Man did not come to be served, but to serve, and to give His life a ransom for many"(Matthew 20:28 NKJV).

When you get on God's elevator, the way up is down. In Matthew 18:4 (NKJV), He says, "Therefore whoever humbles himself as this little child is the greatest in the kingdom of heaven."

There's nothing wrong with being chairman or CEO or wealthy, but the number one priority, goal, and dream of every believer must be to follow Christ at any cost, humbling our-selves to do whatever He asks, putting our agenda second to His. Jesus gave His life that we might live forever, and He says here that we must follow Him, not necessarily to the agonizing death He experienced, but to the death of our own desires, sub-stituting God's plan for our lives.

It's scary to yield our personal goals and wants as we surren-der to Christ, but He promised that giving up our personal ambitions in favor of His plans will not be a problem. "Seek the kingdom of God, and all these things shall be added to you" (Luke 12:31 NKJV).

If we do as He asks, surrendering all we are and have to Him, He will take care of us and provide. And our lives will produce a rich crop that will last a lot longer than our earthly successes.

What about You? Where are you planted? Are you serving God where you know in your heart He has called you? Or are you chasing your own dreams and ambitions and giving Him your leftover time and resources?

SECTION 1: MAKER OF MY LIFE

Spend some time today in prayer, turning over every facet of your life, family, job, and possessions to Him and asking Him to produce a rich crop of righteousness in your life.

Take a Look Read 1 Corinthians 3:5-9 to find out our part and God's part in growing spiritual crops.

COMING HOME

 Let not your heart be troubled; you believe in God, believe also in Me. In My Father's house are many mansions; if it were not so, I would have told you. I go to prepare a place for you. And if I go and prepare a place for you, I will come again and receive you to Myself; that where I am, there you may be also. John 14:1-3 NKJV

BILLY GRAHAM SAID, "Every person needs three homes: a family home; a heavenly home; and a church home." The family home is supposed to be a refuge where a child is nurtured and cared for, a place from which he can venture out into the world more and more as he grows up. A church home is another place to belong and grow strong in relationships with other believers. But whatever a family home or a church home may lack, all believers can look forward to the heavenly home Jesus is preparing for us. Our heavenly home will lack nothing, and it will be more wonderful than we can imagine.

Time after time people close to death have made statements such as, "I'm seeing things too wonderful to describe." Dr. R. G. Lee, pastor of Bellevue Baptist Church in Memphis, Tennessee, said just before his death, "I saw heaven. I can't describe it, but I never did it justice in my preaching." Psalm 16:11 (NKJV) says, "In Your presence is fullness of joy; at Your right hand are pleasures forevermore." Heaven will be grand because of the presence of God.

Home is an important concept and occupies a large place in our memories, our longings, and our dreams. Home represents both the good and bad about family, but it is always a place that draws us back.

According to Abraham Maslow's hierarchy of needs, the need for shelter is one of our most basic needs, ranking with other physical requirements for water, air, and food. He believed that human beings cannot move up to higher level functioning until their needs at each need level are met. For example, a person who is lacking water, air, food, or shelter is struggling merely to survive, and his focus is strictly on meeting those needs. Once those needs are met, he can set out to attain higher level needs such as security and safety, followed by needs for love, affection, and a sense of belonging. Still higher level needs are the need for esteem—self-esteem and the esteem of others. At the top of the hierarchy are needs for self-actualization, which means fulfilling one's purpose in life and helping others, and spiritual needs. Maslow would agree with Billy Graham as to the importance of home.

But the National Coalition for the Homeless estimates that between seven and eight hundred thousand people are homeless on any given night in America. During a year in this country, 2.5 to 3.5 million people will experience homelessness, and about 40 percent are couples or parents with children. These millions of people are struggling to survive, and their attention is simply focused on meeting their most basic needs.

It is urgent that, while we must work to help these unfortunate people find housing and jobs, we also must let them and others know that, regardless of their earthly circumstances, they can be assured of mansions in heaven, prepared for them by Jesus. It will be a place of joyful reunion, total healing, intense beauty, and the deepest satisfaction.

While our earthly home is important, it won't last forever. But we can take comfort in the fact that Jesus is already in our permanent home—our real home—getting it all ready for our arrival.

What about You? What do you think of when you think of home? Do you have good memories or bad ones? And what about reaching your real home in heaven with God? Are you anticipating it with joy, remembering that we are just passing through this world?

SECTION 1: MAKER OF MY LIFE

Take a few minutes to think about heaven and its wonders. Of course, we want to stay in this life as long as we can, but contemplating the glorious mansions in store for us can give us a glimpse of the marvelous times ahead.

Take a Look Read Hebrews 11:13-16 for more about the attitude we should have regarding our time on earth.

A TRIP TO THE ORCHARD

 Abide in Me, and I in you. As the branch cannot bear fruit of itself, unless it abides in the vine, neither can you, unless you abide in Me. I am the vine, you are the branches. He who abides in Me, and I in him, bears much fruit; for without Me you can do nothing. John 15:4-5 NKJV

WHAT DO YOU THINK of when you hear a churchy word like *abide?* Do old-fashioned songs float through your mind ("Abide with me: fast falls the eventide"), making you wonder what that word actually means?

The word *abide* means "to dwell or reside." It also can mean "to last and endure." Jesus drew another clear word picture when He described a branch connected to a vine and said that both need to abide in each other; we need to live in Him and allow Him to live in and through us. If we live in Him, we will endure as His children and followers. We will keep going, and the effects of our lives will last.

Every gardener knows that the green English ivy that seems to live on and on through winters and summers quickly turns brown and dies when clipped from the main vine. The clipped ivy has nothing from which to draw nourishment, and it perishes. That's what abiding in Christ means: staying connected to Him so we have the nourishment and strength to continue living and growing and doing the work He created us to do.

Fruit-bearing is another church word that makes a beautiful picture.

Think of the needs we all have as believers. We need encouragement, faith, teaching, leadership, love, and much more. We see God's methods for meeting those needs in 1 Corinthians 12:7-11:

A spiritual gift is given to each of us as a means of helping the entire church. To one person the Spirit gives the ability to give wise advice; to another he gives the gift of special knowledge. The Spirit gives special faith to another, and to someone else he gives the power to heal the sick. He gives one person the power to perform miracles, and to another the ability to prophesy. He gives someone else the ability to know whether it is really the Spirit of God or another spirit that is speaking. Still another person is given the ability to speak in unknown languages, and another is given the ability to interpret what is being said. It is the one and only Holy Spirit who distributes these gifts. He alone decides which gift each person should have.

Picture an orchard planted with many trees. Each tree is a believer with a particular gift to share with everyone else. When someone needs wise advice, he can go to the wise advice tree; when someone needs her faith strengthened, she can pick fruit from the special faith tree. All of our needs are met in this orchard because God designed it that way. The trees are rooted in the rich soil of the real and living God, Jesus Christ, and from Him they get their nourishment and ability to grow and produce.

Notice that the trees in this orchard, as in any other orchard, aren't stingy with their fruit. In fact, if no one picks and uses the fruit, it falls off and onto the ground to rot and go to waste.

God's plan to provide for His church, the body of Christ, involves each of us. No one is unnecessary or exempt from service. If even one person deprives the rest of the gift he can provide, he creates a lack—an unmet need—in the church, a lack God meant for him to fill.

In God's orchard, every tree is of utmost importance.

What about You? Have you identified your spiritual gifts? If so, are you using them for the benefit of others?

Many churches offer spiritual gift seminars in which believers can identify their spiritual gifts and begin to use them effectively. Ask your church to consider providing this tool for its members, and then be sure to participate when the seminar is scheduled.

Take a Look Read Galatians 5:22-23 and memorize the different types of fruit God desires to develop in our lives.

VANDALISM AND GRAFFITI

 When He, the Spirit of truth, has come, He will guide you into all truth; for He will not speak on His own authority, but whatever He hears He will speak; and He will tell you things to come. He will glorify Me, for He will take of what is Mine and declare it to you. John 16:13-14 NKJV

JESUS' PROMISE that He would send His Spirit after He had left the disciples must have seemed like a lifeline to them. They wanted Him to stay with them, but they knew He must go. Perhaps they thought the Holy Spirit would appear in visible form as Jesus had done, so that He could guide them and speak to them, but that was not the plan. He was to live inside each believer, making Himself personal to each one.

In 1 Corinthians 6:19-20 (NKJV), we read, "Or do you not know that your body is the temple of the Holy Spirit who is in you, whom you have from God, and you are not your own? For you were bought at a price; therefore glorify God in your body and in your spirit, which are God's." Imagine God living in you, making your body His dwelling place.

Now go a step further in your imagination. Approach the magnificent palace in awe. Its gleaming white walls must have been polished just this morning. Its shiny copper cupolas show no discoloration or imperfection. The palace windows gleam, framed by rubies and sapphires. Even the cobbled walkway under your feet is swept clean and every stone is perfect: unchipped and multi-hued.

The twenty-foot-tall oak double doors swing open as you approach, and you enter, holding your breath at the beauty of the place. The inside is even more opulent than the outside, and you find yourself wanting to touch the garnet shelves along the tapestried walls, to stand in the colored lights reflecting down through the stained glass ceiling, to gaze at your surroundings and drink it all in.

But instead of standing calmly in the beauty of the palace, you suddenly grab a candle in a wall sconce and set one of the tapestries on fire. You upend the potted palms dotting the anteroom, scattering dirt over the floor, and you untie the ends of the smelly garbage bag you brought in with you and dump the contents on the polished stone floor. You pull out a small can of red spray paint from your back pocket and splash obscenities on the palace walls.

Why would you act so irrationally? Why would anyone deliberately mar perfection or damage a structure that was obviously well loved and cared for?

When we understand that the human body really is the temple of the Holy Spirit, we can see that behaviors that harm our bodies are as irrational as setting fire to the palace tapestries. Oh, sure, we know that smoking cigarettes is harmful, and taking illegal drugs destroys our health, but what about the poisons we put into our bodies as food or into our minds as entertainment?

Jesus said the Spirit would glorify Him, not desecrate Him with pollution and misuse. Take an inventory of your life and your temple, carefully and honestly rating yourself on your level of care for that important structure.

What about You? What does it mean to you that your body is the temple of God, His dwelling place? Do you respect it, care for it, and take care of it for Him? Or do you mistreat it, neglect it, even hate it?

Ask God to change your heart today and give you a new appreciation for His dwelling place, your body. Ask Him to help you provide fuel and maintenance for your body so that it can continue to glorify Him for many years.

Take a Look Read Romans 12:1 (NKJV). How would you define "holy [and] acceptable to God" when it comes to your body?

THE REAL LORD'S PRAYER

 Father, the hour has come. Glorify Your Son, that Your Son also may glorify You, as You have given Him authority over all flesh, that He should give eternal life to as many as You have given Him. And this is eternal life, that they may know You, the only true God, and Jesus Christ whom You have sent. I have glorified You on the earth. I have finished the work which You have given Me to do. And now, O Father, glorify Me together with Yourself, with the glory which I had with You before the world was. John 17:1-5 NKJV

WE KNOW the Lord's Prayer as the one Jesus used to teach His disciples about prayer in Matthew 6:9-13 (NKJV), beginning, "Our Father in heaven, hallowed be Your name." That beautiful prayer has been and will be prayed by believers throughout the generations.

But the real Lord's Prayer, the one Jesus prayed before His death on the cross, is found in John 17. Jesus had been instructing His disciples in the upper room concerning the future, urging them to be strong in their faith, their relationships with one another, and in prayer. He promised to leave them with the Holy Spirit, and with answered prayer, peace, and joy. At the end of their time together in the upper room or on the road from there to the garden of Gethsemane in the Kidron Valley, Jesus prayed this prayer aloud. It was a conversation between God the Father and God the Son, a conversation that until this time had only been heard in heaven.

As He faced the agony of death on the cross, He prayed for Himself in verses 1 through 5. He then prayed for His disciples in verses 6 through 19, and for all believers of all the ages in verses 20 through 26.

He knew the angry insults and the mocking jeers that were ahead of Him. He understood the anguish of the physical, emotional, and spiritual pain He would experience as He carried the sin of the world to the cross.

And He remembered the glories of heaven that He had left to come to earth. But in this prayer, we don't hear regret or selfishness or defeat. Instead, Jesus realized that His victory was near, that "the hour has come," and He looked beyond the cross. The author of Hebrews writes, ". . . who for the joy that was set before Him endured the cross, despising the shame, and has sat down at the right hand of the throne of God" (Hebrews 12:2 NKJV).

In what has been called Jesus' high priestly prayer, He prayed that, as He finished the work God had given Him to do, God would be glorified. He didn't list His accomplishments or say there were a few healings or miracles He hadn't found time to do yet. His desire was simply that people would know God through His life and death, and by knowing Him would have eternal life.

When we give our lives to Jesus, we immediately possess eternal life. Eternal life begins here and now, not when we die and go to heaven. If we don't have eternal life when we get to eternity, it will be too late—too late to take that all-important step of faith toward Jesus Christ. He will take it from there, magnifying Himself in your life as you live in obedience and faith.

As He faced the cross, He prayed for Himself and His disciples, and He also prayed for you and me, which He continues to do today.

Think of Jesus just outside the door of your room, or through the wall in the room next to yours, talking to God the Father specifically about Your needs. If you knew He were ten feet from you, talking to God on your behalf, it would be a lot easier to have confidence that God is in control of all things. And that's exactly the situation. Hebrews 7:25 says, "He lives forever to plead with God on their behalf."

In the real Lord's Prayer, Jesus faced the torment of the cross, but today His agony is over; His pain is done. The victory is won for us so that we, too, can live to glorify God.

What about You? Does eternal life seem like something way out in the distant future, or do you live each day as part of the long continuum from here to forever? Is your goal in line with Jesus' goal expressed in His high priestly prayer—glorifying God so that many will know Him?

Realizing that Jesus is actually closer than if He were in the next room praying for you, what would you ask Him to bring before the Father on your behalf? Would your request be for help so that your prayer could be like Jesus', to glorify God in your life so that more people could know Him?

Take a Look First Corinthians 10:31-32 talks about areas of life in which we are to glorify God. Read that and then list three additional ways you can seek to glorify God in your life.

THE BREVITY OF LIFE

 Jesus' trial before Caiaphas ended in the early hours of the morning. Then he was taken to the headquarters of the Roman governor. John 18:28

BILLY GRAHAM has said that one of the most surprising things he's observed about life is how fast it goes by—the brevity of life. With each passing year, the clock and the calendar seem to speed up until it seems as if birthdays come every month instead of once a year.

Jesus' earthly life was brief by twenty-first century standards. Thirty-three is very young today. But that final night during His unjust trial must have seemed very long indeed. One way to slow down the clock is to go through difficulty or pain. Days spent sick in the hospital can seem endless. As Jesus neared the cross, we wonder if time slowed for Him. Before Him was the picture of returning to heaven after defeating death and the grave, but the road leading there was one of agony.

Jesus' life was brief but filled with accomplishment during His short three-year public ministry. He healed the sick, forgave sinners, fed the multitudes, and turned water into wine.

He preached a new message of love and forgiveness. He raised the status of women as He spoke to the outcast woman at the well and sent those who would condemn the adulterous woman away. He exposed the falseness of legalistic, self-righteous religion. And He pointed the true way to God.

In His greatest act, Jesus went to the cross to pay for sin and to destroy death forever. His short life forever changed history.

God has created each person with a purpose, a role only he or she can play in history. He puts that desire into each heart and equips the person to fulfill that role. Each human life, whether long or short, has a unique purpose. But we must pursue it and work to achieve it with God's help.

Second Thessalonians 1:11-12 says, "And so we keep on praying for you, that our God will make you worthy of the life to which he called you. And we pray that God, by his power, will fulfill all your good intentions and faithful deeds. Then everyone will give honor to the name of our Lord Jesus because of you, and you will be honored along with him. This is all made possible because of the undeserved favor of our God and Lord, Jesus Christ."

Our real purpose is to bring honor to the name of Jesus, fulfilling the unique role God gave each person. As Mordecai asked Queen Esther, who was to risk her life to save her people, "Who can say but that you have been elevated to the palace for just such a time as this?" (Esther 4:14).

God brought you to where you are in life for just this time in history, a time to serve Him as only you can do.

What about You? What have you accomplished in life so far? Do you have specific goals that you believe God wants to fulfill in your life? Do you have a plan to attain those goals or are you just counting on things to take care of themselves as you meander through life?

Get out your list of goals, and if you don't have one ask God to show you what He wants to accomplish through you. Write down at least three goals and one action step for each that will head you in the direction of accomplishing them.

Take a Look Look up Numbers 9:23 and Joshua 24:24-28 and find a key ingredient in discovering God's purpose for one's life.

HANGING ON

Jesus said to her, "Woman, why are you weeping? Whom are you seeking?" She, supposing Him to be the gardener, said to Him, "Sir, if You have carried Him away, tell me where You have laid Him, and I will take Him away." Jesus said to her, "Mary!" She turned and said to Him, "Rabboni!" (which is to say, Teacher). Jesus said to her, "Do not cling to Me, for I have not yet ascended to My Father; but go to My brethren and say to them, 'I am ascending to My Father and your Father, and to My God and your God.'" John 20:15-17 NKJV

MARY desperately held on to Jesus, wanting to keep Him with her forever. In the past, she had been demon-possessed and immoral in a culture that scorned such women. She had finally found a friend in Jesus, who had treated her with dignity and who had forgiven her. She was a new woman because of this marvelous man, and now she was afraid she had lost Him. She must have clung with all her strength when He appeared to her in the garden because she never wanted to let Him slip away again.

Mary's love was great, unlike the Pharisees who felt no need for forgiveness. After all, they kept the law, of which they were so knowledgeable. Jesus said of people like Mary who know their need for Him and find it met, "I tell you, her sins—and they are many—have been forgiven, so she has shown me much love. But a person who is forgiven little shows only little love" (Luke 7:47).

Jesus honored Mary by appearing first to her, but He also redefined their relationship in John 20. No longer would it be based on physical sight and touch. Instead, the new relationship would be real and powerful, but not shared in one another's physical presence. It would be based on faith instead of feelings, but it was no less genuine.

In explaining the change to Mary, Jesus also made it clear for us. Our relationship with Him transcends His physical presence; we experience Him through the Holy Spirit by faith.

Mary's heart cry was "Why the heartache, Lord? Is this the end? Is life just a senseless experience of pain and eventual death?" Jesus met her need, and ours, with something greater, larger than physical sight and experience. He rose from the dead and went to be with His Father so that the Spirit could come and help each believer. No longer would Mary only be able to experience Jesus when she could see Him with her eyes or cling to Him with her arms. Now she could be with Him every hour of every day, forever.

What about You? Do you wish Jesus would simply speak audibly to you and let you know what He wants you to do? Do you wish you could just see Him one time and then you'd be sure He's there?

In John 20:29 Jesus told Thomas it was better to believe without having to see proof. Join the man with the demon-possessed son in Mark 9:24 (NKJV) when he said, "Lord, I believe; help my unbelief!"

Take a Look Read 1 Corinthians 2:9-16. Find at least two ways the Holy Spirit gives believers more than what we can see with our physical eyes.

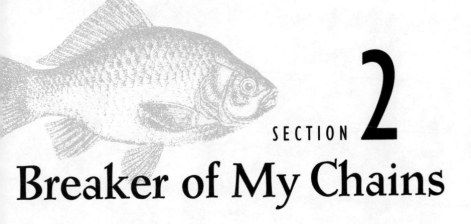

SECTION 2

Breaker of My Chains

THE COURAGE TO CHANGE

 John pointed him out to the people. He shouted to the crowds, "This is the one I was talking about when I said, 'Someone is coming who is far greater than I am, for he existed long before I did.'" John 1:15

MANY YEARS AGO, Bill was an alcoholic who wanted no part of church. His wife, Maureen, tried again and again to get him to go to church with her, and finally one Saturday evening thirteen years ago, he gave in and dragged himself to church. Bill just wanted to sit through the service and get out as fast as he could. The sermon focused on the bondage of alcoholism and other addictions. Bill could have hardened his heart and left the church unchanged. But he sensed God speaking to him, and he went home and prayed, asking God to forgive him and make Jesus his Savior. He has been free of alcohol ever since. Many times he has had to ask God to help him develop the discipline needed to overcome his habit, and on every occasion God has come through.

As we look at John the Baptist's life, we see the importance of discipline, devotion, and determination. From these three qualities grew the freedom John had to proclaim Christ.

Some people thought of John as a freak, a fool, or a fanatic, but he didn't care. He wanted only to point people to Jesus, and he did that boldly. He set aside everything in his life in order to do the job God called him to. He didn't drink alcohol (Luke 1:15), and he was filled with the Holy Spirit. He kept his eyes focused on God as he lived alone in the wilderness, eating simply and growing strong. John avoided entanglements with the hypocritical religious leaders of his day. He was a disciplined man.

John was also devoted to God. Even before his birth, an angel told his parents of God's important work for their coming son.

"He will precede the coming of the Lord, preparing the people for his arrival. He will turn the hearts of the fathers to their children, and he will change disobedient minds to accept godly wisdom" (Luke 1:17). He was a prophet much like the Old Testament prophets who foretold of the coming Messiah.

And John was determined—determined to point people to Jesus, no matter what the cost to himself. He knew that the world needed a savior. He magnified Christ and minimized John. He preached repentance and confronted the powerful. He knew his role and he made up his mind to fulfill it.

The result of John's personal discipline, his sold-out devotion, and his steely determination was that he pleased God. "For I say to you, among those born of women there is not a greater prophet than John the Baptist" (Luke 7:28 NKJV).

John displayed the reality of Christ. Unafraid to boldly proclaim Him, John announced that the real Savior had come.

What about You? Are you disciplined, free from things that would control you? Are you devoted to God, putting Him first in your life, ahead of your own ambition and desires? Are you determined to follow God's leading in your life, even if it costs you comfort, money, or time?

Ask God to make you a willing follower, an obedient servant, a self-controlled believer. He provided John with the strength to persevere in the face of opposition, to stay true to Christ even until John's death, and to call many to repentance and faith in his beloved Messiah. He'll do it for you, too.

Take a Look Read 2 Peter 1:5-8 and diagram the progression in the believer's life from faith to usefulness. What is the role of self-control in this sequence?

FREE TO BE SECOND

 The next day John saw Jesus coming toward him and said, "Look! There is the Lamb of God who takes away the sin of the world!" John 1:29

SECOND FIDDLE. Has-been. Warm-up act. For many people, riding on the coattails of another can be ego-deflating. But for others, the joy of just being in the show is enough.

The Sweet Inspirations performed as a warm-up act for Elvis Presley back in 1970. Their job was to get the audience ready for the star. They knew the crowd was really there to see Elvis, and that was acceptable to singers Ann, Myrna, Sylvia, and Estelle.

Of course we can't compare Elvis with Jesus or the Sweet Inspirations with John the Baptist, but essentially John served as the warm-up act for Jesus, and that role was acceptable to him. He considered himself unworthy even to untie Jesus' sandals (John 1:26-27), but he was passionate about getting the people ready for Jesus.

John preached like no other before him. He had a huge following of his own, and he baptized thousands. When the Pharisees sent priests and Levites to investigate whether John was the Messiah and find out why he was so popular, John knew they came with suspicion, rather than a sincere desire to follow Jesus. His response was simple, yet profound, as he explained that he was only there to make a pathway for the Lord.

The next day, the very purpose of John's life was crystallized in his announcement, "Look! There is the Lamb of God who takes away the sin of the world!" He deflected the attention from himself and onto the true Messiah, Jesus.

He pointed people to Jesus, stepping aside and exiting the limelight. He was willing for his great life to be eclipsed by the greater life of Christ. He knew the desperate need of the people for Christ and burned with an intensity to introduce them to Jesus, to lead them to repentance that they might be set free of their sins.

He cried out in the wilderness, and we know by the words John used that he literally "howled." He howled with intensity, and he stepped aside with humility. His only goal was to prepare the way for the Lord who came to change hearts and set people free.

You, too, have a purpose, a job to do for God that only you can do. But before you can embark on that journey, you must get free. The first words of Jesus in Mark's gospel were: "The kingdom of God is at hand. Repent, and believe in the gospel" (Mark 1:15 NKJV). And in Luke 13:3 (NKJV), He said, "But unless you repent you will all likewise perish."

Repentance means to change direction, and if you truly change directions, Jesus will change your heart as well. That doesn't mean that you even know what all of your sins are so you can confess them. It means that as you read God's Word, God will shine His light on your areas of sin and weakness and rebellion, showing you where you need to repent. He will transform you from the inside out, breaking the chains that hold you and setting you free.

Repentance is not perfection, but it's a sincere desire to live in obedience to God. False repentance lacks sincerity. Think of it this way: You're driving down the road and you get pulled over for speeding. You tell the officer that you're very sorry. But if the policeman lets you go, and you drive away and start speeding again, you were actually just sorry for getting caught. You didn't repent and change your ways because you weren't sincerely sorry for what you had done.

John's life shows us that greatness and humility go hand in hand, and that freedom and repentance are supernatural companions. John preached boldly, but he stepped aside quietly. He led others; but he followed Jesus.

SECTION 2: BREAKER OF MY CHAINS

What about You? Are you able to do your work or service or ministry behind the scenes, offstage, out of sight? Are you free from the need for recognition or praise or accolade? Follow John as he points others to Jesus, focusing the attention away from himself and onto God.

Take a Look Read what the Lord says to the church in Philadelphia in Revelation 3:7-12. That church is not mighty in strength or free from difficulty; yet it is affirmed for its obedience and endurance. What characteristics does this church share with John the Baptist?

PERFECT PASSION

 Jesus made a whip from some ropes and chased them all out of the Temple. He drove out the sheep and oxen, scattered the money changers' coins over the floor, and turned over their tables. Then, going over to the people who sold doves, he told them, "Get these things out of here. Don't turn my Father's house into a marketplace!" John 2:15-16

JESUS WAS A MAN of heartfelt emotion, not a pasty, expressionless fellow who walked around stone-faced. He experienced the feelings that all of us have, including both anger and joy, which can seem like opposite ends of the spectrum.

In John 2 we see a very angry Jesus. The Temple was crowded with out-of-town visitors during Passover. It was also packed with merchants trying to make money from the worshipers. This majestic place of worship featured marble walls and golden columns. The court of the Gentiles, where all nations were welcomed, was 250 yards wide—about the size of three football fields.

Jesus didn't like what He saw going on there. He was angry at the religious crowd, the hypocrites who were cheating the people of God by charging them high prices for the sacrifices they needed to purchase after traveling long distances. The worshipers also had to exchange their Roman or Greek coins for the official religious coins, and this provided a profit as well.

Jesus losing His temper was not a mere emotional outburst. It was a planned and decisive action. He took the time to make a whip. And then He began to clean up the Temple, driving out the corruption. Although He was angry, He did not sin, which is a human temptation at times of anger.

In addition to feeling anger, Jesus was also a man of joy. He spoke of His joy in John 15:10-11: "When you obey me, you remain in my love, just as I obey my Father and remain in his love. I have told you this so that you will be filled with my joy. Yes, your joy will overflow!"

Jesus radiated the life and love of God. There was joy at His birth as the angels announced His arrival (Luke 2:10) and joy at His baptism that God the Father showed when He said, "This is My beloved Son, in whom I am well pleased" (2 Peter 1:17 NKJV). There was joy when Jesus called His followers to leave their nets and follow Him, when He healed the sick, when He made the leper clean, when He forgave the adulterous woman, and when the stone was rolled away and the angel announced, "He is not here; for He is risen" (Matthew 28:6 NKJV). Everywhere Jesus is, there joy is also.

So why are we often so glum? Church shouldn't be stale and stodgy and cold and dark and serious. That's not Jesus at all. In Him, there is freedom, openness, and transparency. He attracted all kinds of people because the glow of God shone upon Him. He came to share the joy of knowing Him. The gospel message is "Good News," not bad news or boring news or sad news.

Jesus showed us that there is nothing wrong with happiness and laughter. More than any other people, Christians have a reason to be joyful. We know the true Source of joy. Jesus also proved that there are times when controlled anger is the appropriate response, as when we see injustice and sin. Controlled anger can provide the energy and motivation to act on behalf of the poor, to try to right wrongs done to a defenseless person, or to lovingly confront a friend ensnared in sinful patterns.

Jesus showed us that our God-given emotions are not wrong; what counts is how we handle our feelings.

What about You? What is your passion level? Do you experience joy and anger, as well as all the other emotions God gave us? Or are you indifferent, cynical, and bored? Sometimes it's too painful to experience our feelings and we shut them down.

But in doing that, we rob ourselves and our loved ones of the fullness of life, a life lived with passion.

Join Jesus today and give yourself permission to experience both the joy of knowing Him and the anger He felt at hypocrisy and greed. The next time you experience one of these emotions, use your feelings to prompt you to action on behalf of others.

Take a Look Read Psalm 30, David's song about how God's anger lasts for just a moment, but His favor for a lifetime (verse 5), and how He turns our weeping into joy (verse 11). Find two additional ways God helps those who call on Him.

THE FAITH CONNECTION

When he heard that Jesus had come from Judea and was traveling in Galilee, he went over to Cana. He found Jesus and begged him to come to Capernaum with him to heal his son, who was about to die. John 4:47

ONE OF THE GREATEST pitchers in baseball was Jim "Catfish" Hunter. As he was dying from Lou Gehrig's disease, the fifty-three-year-old former player said, "I would give all of the accolades, the applause, all the World Series victories, the Cy Young Award, everything I have achieved in baseball, everything I've received in life, for my health." He knew what the nobleman in John 4 knew: the value of physical health.

This nobleman served as a civil servant in either the household or government of Herod Antipas. He had position, power, and prestige. But he knew that all his power and wealth could do nothing to heal his son who was desperately ill.

The man knew of Jesus, perhaps because of the great uproar in Jerusalem over His astounding words and miraculous healings. The nobleman had likely heard of the power exhibited in Jesus' life. As often happens with us today, this man had a serious problem, and he went to Jesus for help. Problems often propel people to Jesus. The nobleman's desperation drove him to Jesus, and he begged Him to heal his son. His pain led to his first step of faith, just as heartbreak, darkness, and trouble can point us in the direction of God.

We try to avoid pain or take measures to avoid it. But without his pain, this man might never have come to Jesus. The same is true for us. We think a pain-free existence would be wonderful, but pain is an advantage if it helps us come to Christ.

In their book, *The Gift of Pain,* Philip Yancey and Paul Brand show clearly that the ability to feel pain is a gift from God. Dr. Brand's medical career was devoted to the care of lepers, and his patients' inability to feel pain is what injured them the most. They couldn't tell when an activity was harming their hands or feet, for example, so they took no steps to stop the damage. Similarly, without pain and difficulty in life, people tend to think of themselves as self-sufficient without a need for God. They, too, become numb to their true needs.

But not this nobleman. His pain pushed him in Jesus' direction; he cried out in faith and connected with God. His faith was small at first. He just wanted a miracle for his son. Any good parent can relate to his feelings. You would do anything to help your child. Pain can prod us toward the Savior, as it did a father named Alan.

The last thing Alan expected was to lose his job. He had worked at the company for ten years and had been a high producer every year. His income had grown nicely, and he assumed he would continue on this career path indefinitely. None of the employees knew about the merger until the end of work on Friday when they were given thick envelopes containing explanations of each person's severance package.

During nine months of job-hunting, Alan realized that it was not his ability or his hard work that had gotten him where he had been. As he faced the possible loss of the family's home, he saw that every gift was from the hand of God, including the ability and opportunity to work. Alan's pain drove him to God. By the time he landed a new position, the source of his confidence had shifted from himself to Jesus.

What about You? What do you do when you find yourself in physical, spiritual, or emotional pain? Do you see pain as something to be avoided at all costs, a condition to get through as quickly as possible? Do you try to numb yourself to your pain through frantic activity or by ingesting a substance like alcohol or drugs? Or do you allow your pain to push you in the direc-

tion of Jesus who longs to help you bear it? Follow the nobleman, find Jesus, and beg Him to come and help you. I promise
you He will.

Take a Look Read the story of the crippled woman who cried
out to Jesus in Luke 13:10-17. She, too, allowed her pain to
drive her boldly to Jesus to ask for help. What was His response
to the religious leaders' criticism?

GETTING WELL

 Now a certain man was there who had an infirmity thirty-eight years. When Jesus saw him lying there, and knew that he already had been in that condition a long time, He said to him, "Do you want to be made well?" The sick man answered Him, "Sir, I have no man to put me into the pool when the water is stirred up; but while I am coming, another steps down before me." Jesus said to him, "Rise, take up your bed and walk." John 5:5-8 NKJV

WHY WOULD ANYONE want to remain sick? Wanting to be sick sounds sick, doesn't it? And yet Jesus asked the sick man in John 5 whether he wanted to be made well. Anyone would want to get well, wouldn't they?

Not necessarily, according to Jesus. Sometimes we use sickness as an excuse to avoid doing what God has called us to do. Sickness can be an excuse for not working or helping around the house. It can be an excuse for refusing to show hospitality to others. It can be used to avoid social contact.

Some people get lung cancer or liver disease because of their choices to smoke or to abuse alcohol or drugs. They want to be well, but often the addiction is more powerful than their desire for health.

In a sense, all sickness is the result of sin that entered the world when Adam and Eve sinned. Of course, not everyone who is sick wants to be, and not all sickness is the result of a person's sin. The righteous suffer also. The apostle Paul was sick, praying three times for God to deliver him. But God's answer was no. "My grace is sufficient for you"(2 Corinthians 12:9 NKJV). Many godly people today also suffer from cancer and other diseases.

The man in John 5 was helpless after being sick for thirty-eight years. He couldn't even get himself down into the pool.

Jesus singled him out from all the others in need of healing. We don't know why God heals some people on this side of heaven and others not until eternity. But Jesus might have chosen this man because he was in the most helpless condition of anyone, and there would be no doubt when Jesus healed him that the power of God was at work. But before healing the man, Jesus asked if he wanted to be healed because He never forces Himself on anyone. Perhaps the man wouldn't want to take the responsibility of a life of wholeness.

Jesus knew the man needed more than a miracle; he needed the Messiah. Jesus said to the paralyzed man as He says to us today, "Rise, take up your bed and walk." He asked him to make a break from his past, to pick up his cot, break the chains, and follow Christ.

The man had to respond in faith to the power of Jesus, who always enables us to fulfill His commandments. If He tells us to do something, He gives us the ability to do it. The man simply needed to believe and stand, proving Jesus to be reliable and true.

You may feel helpless like the paralyzed man, like you just can't change yourself or your situation. But sometimes helpless is the best way to be. Lifeguards sometimes need to wait until a drowning person has stopped flailing, fighting, and panicking before he can be rescued. When we come to the end of ourselves, admitting our helplessness, we begin to find God.

What about You? Do you want to be made well? Do you want healed relationships, healthy attitudes, freedom from bad habits? Or are you comfortable in your present situation? Miserable, but comfortable?

Jesus makes the same offer to you today that He made to the sick man. "Get up, break free, and follow Me." Will you do it, taking Him at His word and responding in faith?

Take a Look Read Colossians 1:9-12. Find at least four specific things Paul is asking God to give to believers.

THE LIFESAVER

 Most assuredly, I say to you, he who hears My word and believes in Him who sent Me has everlasting life, and shall not come into judgment, but has passed from death into life.
John 5:24 NKJV

FEAR GRIPPED LAURIE as she dialed the help-line number. Seventeen and pregnant, she hadn't told her parents yet. Her boyfriend had left for college right after she told him the news, encouraging her just to "take care of it" with an abortion. She had withdrawn money from her savings account, money she had earned as a cashier after school, and made an appointment at the clinic for the next day. But before she went to the clinic, Laurie just wanted to talk to someone who might understand.

Diane, the crisis pregnancy counselor, told Laurie she had been in the same situation five years earlier. As she talked, Laurie began to calm down, wondering if it was possible that there was a way out of this mess. Diane told Laurie that someone had introduced her to Jesus right before her planned abortion, and she had decided to give birth and place her baby for adoption. It had been hard, but Diane knew she had done the right thing.

Laurie felt like a lifeline had been thrown to her—and to her unborn child. Her hands shook as she dialed the clinic to cancel her appointment, but now they shook with excitement instead of fear.

Laurie chose life over death, and that's what Christ offers to all who will come. New life—a fuller, better life. Real life as God intended it.

Death surrounds us today. Violence, war, and terrorism confront us daily on the news. But few people in history have experienced the level of tragedy that God's servant Job did. We

shudder when we read of the sudden loss of all seven of Job's
sons and three daughters on one terrible day, every parent's
worst nightmare—losing not just one child, but all of them.

Next, Job lost his wealth, possessions, and even his servants.
Finally, his health was taken, and everything he had was gone.
In a sense, he even lost his friends and his wife, who turned
against him in his hour of need. Understandably, he wished he
had never been born. But even as he grieved and suffered, the
Bible says he did not sin by charging God with wrongdoing (Job
1:22 NIV). He cried out to God in his pain, and God's answer
was all about life.

In Job 38 and 39, God displays His life-giving power as He
questions Job, "Where were you when I laid the earth's foundation? Do you give the horse his strength or clothe his neck with
a flowing mane? Who provides food for the raven when its
young cry out to God and wander about for lack of food? Does
the hawk take flight by your wisdom?"

Job wisely replied, "I know that You can do everything, and
that no purpose of Yours can be withheld from You. You asked,
'Who is this who hides counsel without knowledge?' Therefore
I have uttered what I did not understand, things too wonderful
for me, which I did not know" (Job 42:2-3 NKJV).

Job chose life over death as he submitted to God's sovereignty. He didn't have all the answers, but he knew the One
who did, the one and only true God.

What about You? Will you choose life over death today? Will
you put all your questions and doubts and worries into the
hand of the One whose plans cannot be thwarted? He offers to
turn your mourning into dancing, to restore your joy as He did
for Job. Look up, and let Him do that for you.

Take a Look "The unfailing love of the LORD never ends! By
his mercies we have been kept from complete destruction.
Great is his faithfulness; his mercies begin afresh each day. I say

to myself, 'The LORD is my inheritance; therefore, I will hope in him!'"(Lamentations 3:22-24).

List three ways you or your family have been kept from destruction, accident, tragedy, or loss, as you have experienced God's mercy and protection. Perhaps He helped you, too, make a life-giving choice. Thank Him for that today.

OPEN-HANDED LIVING

 Then they said to Him, "What shall we do, that we may work the works of God?" Jesus answered and said to them, "This is the work of God, that you believe in Him whom He sent." Therefore they said to Him, "What sign will You perform then, that we may see it and believe You? What work will You do? Our fathers ate the manna in the desert; as it is written, 'He gave them bread from heaven to eat.'"
John 6:28-31 NKJV

WHEN YOU DON'T have much money, giving a portion of your income to church can be hard to do. After Kristin lost her job at the technology company, it took her more than a year to find a new position, and even then, her salary was lower than it had been in her previous job. Six months into the new job she hadn't been able to pay off all her debts that had piled up when she wasn't working, and she hadn't been giving to her church because she felt she really needed to climb out of debt first.

But she decided to tithe a tenth of her next paycheck, regardless of her indebtedness. On payday, she quickly wrote out a check for two hundred dollars before she changed her mind. *Boy, that could go a long way toward paying off my credit card debt,* she thought. On Sunday she put the check into the offering basket, asking God to meet her needs as He always had.

On Monday, Kristin's car wouldn't start and she had to have it towed to the repair shop. The new battery cost nearly one hundred dollars. On Wednesday, she learned that the dental work she needed would cost several hundred dollars, despite her insurance coverage. Kristin began to wonder if she had done the right thing in giving her check at church on Sunday.

On Friday evening after Kristin got home from work, the doorbell rang and she was surprised to find her friend Denise at the door. As the women hugged each other, Denise said, "Are you okay? I felt as if I really needed to come see you and bring you this." She handed Kristin a check for almost exactly what her donation had been.

Kristin had to sit down as she realized that once again, God had met her needs in a surprising way. He provided a sign of the reality of His care for her.

Of course, there's no guarantee that God will always give us back money we give to Him. But He loves a cheerful giver (2 Corinthians 9:7), and Luke 6:38 says, "If you give, you will receive. Your gift will return to you in full measure, pressed down, shaken together to make room for more, and running over. Whatever measure you use in giving—large or small—it will be used to measure what is given back to you."

He also promises to provide for us. Philippians 4:19 (NKJV) says, "And my God shall supply all your need according to His riches in glory by Christ Jesus." We sometimes get our needs confused with our wants, but God knows what we truly need, in both the material and spiritual realm, and He provides it.

In John 6:28-30 the crowd challenged Jesus to perform another miracle, referring to God's miraculous provision of manna when the Israelites wandered in the desert. They missed the all-important distinction between bread and Bread, and Jesus patiently explained again that He is God's true provision for all human needs.

What about You? Are you able to trust that God will provide what you need? Are you able to hold your material possessions and your money loosely, generously giving to Christian ministries and to those in need?

Test God in your giving. Give to Him and see what He brings in the way of both spiritual blessings and material provision.

Take a Look Read the story of God's amazing care for the widow in 1 Kings 17:8-24. What can you learn about the link between faith, obedience, and God's provision?

RIGHT OR WRONG

 So when they continued asking Him, He raised Himself up and said to them, "He who is without sin among you, let him throw a stone at her first." And again He stooped down and wrote on the ground. Then those who heard it, being convicted by their conscience, went out one by one, beginning with the oldest even to the last. And Jesus was left alone, and the woman standing in the midst. John 8:7-9 NKJV

THE YOUNG BOY brought the small broken porcelain statue to his mother. He said, "I wanted to hide this so you wouldn't know I knocked it over, Mom, but my conscience wouldn't let me do it."

The boy's conscience was tender and sensitive to right and wrong. And it plagued him when he tried to hide wrongdoing. Our conscience is that inner sense of what is right or wrong in our conduct that impels us toward right action. But the Bible says our consciences can be destroyed by prolonged sin. "These teachers are hypocrites and liars. They pretend to be religious, but their consciences are dead" (1 Timothy 4:2).

Sometimes the greatest sinners are the ones who criticize others the most. Angry people often overlook their own imperfections, but they constantly harp on the flaws of others. But evidently, the crowd who accused the adulterous woman in John 8 still had their consciences intact.

There has been much speculation as to what Jesus wrote on the ground in this passage. Some say He wrote the Ten Commandments or perhaps a portion of the Sermon on the Mount, such as Matthew 5:28 (NKJV), "But I say to you that whoever looks at a woman to lust for her has already committed adultery with her in his heart." Or perhaps He wrote the secret sins of her accusers. Josephus and other historians wrote that many of the religious leaders in Jerusalem were particularly immoral.

It seems that what we cover, God uncovers; and what we uncover, God covers. If we hide our sins in secret compartments of our lives instead of confessing them, God will eventually uncover them. But if we confess our sins and repent, God will cover our sin with His love.

Jesus did both in this situation. Rather than rendering a quick judgment, He waited, writing on the ground. He didn't judge rashly. Jesus, who came from the majesty of heaven, stooped down to write in the dirt. In Romans 2:1 (NKJV), Paul says, "Therefore you are inexcusable, O man, whoever you are who judge, for in whatever you judge another you condemn yourself; for you who judge practice the same things." Jesus, the only one legitimately qualified to judge others, refused to do it here.

Whatever He wrote on the ground that day convicted those standing there, reminding them of their own guilt. Their consciences told them to drop their stones and walk away.

What about You? What's the condition of your conscience? Is it alive and well, prodding you toward right action? Or is it deadened from disuse? Or perhaps your conscience is overly strict, making you feel guilty when you do something as innocent as saying no to a request for a commitment you don't have time to fulfill.

Ask God to renew your conscience and cause it to work properly so that you will have a true sense of right and wrong and always move in the direction of doing right.

Take a Look Read Romans 5:16-17 and contrast the results of Adam's sin and Christ's payment for sin. Write down one or two characteristics of the gift Jesus provided.

FREE TO GO

 When Jesus had raised Himself up and saw no one but the woman, He said to her, "Woman, where are those accusers of yours? Has no one condemned you?" She said, "No one, Lord." And Jesus said to her, "Neither do I condemn you; go and sin no more." John 8:10-11 NKJV

WHAT WAS the adulterous woman thinking as they dragged her before Jesus? *It's over. I'm dead, done for, at the point of no return. There's no forgiveness for me.* She probably thought God was angry with her. She knew the punishment for adultery was stoning. The circumstances of her sin are unknown, and the man involved is not mentioned. But we know the situation was a setup so that the religious leaders could bring her before Jesus and try to trip Him up in His response to her. The leaders thought He would make a mistake and contradict either the law of Moses that required her to be stoned or His own message of love and forgiveness. Either way, they would be able to discredit Him.

But their tactics failed. Perfectly consistent, Jesus did not condemn her. He knew that He was on His way to the cross to accept her judgment along with yours and mine. Notice that Jesus didn't say, "Go and live a sinless life and then maybe I'll forgive you." Many religions say, "Clean up your life, do certain religious acts, and maybe God will forgive you and let you into heaven." That's the opposite of what Jesus did. First He loved and forgave her, setting her free. Only then did He tell her to obey God. There's nothing we can do to make ourselves more acceptable to God. He accepts us only when we come to Him just as we are: honestly, sincerely, and without pretense.

Finally she was alone with Him, as we will all be one day when we stand before Him. She didn't make up excuses or try to justify her actions or blame someone else. She merely acknowledged who He was by calling Him "Lord." Not rabbi or teacher, but Lord. Her response to His love and forgiveness was simple faith.

The world is full of broken people like this woman. They think God is angry at them and they can never be forgiven. Christ's message is one of mercy. He chose the sinners and outcasts, not the religious leaders or the churchgoers as His people. Even the sin of adultery couldn't keep this woman out of heaven; even the Pharisees' religion couldn't get them in. He was known as the true friend of sinners. Jesus sought out the despised people—the tax collectors, the prostitutes, the lepers. He welcomed those who did not know God. He talked to them about the love of God, "For God did not send His Son into the world to condemn the world, but that the world through Him might be saved" (John 3:17 NKJV).

What about You? What is your response to people trapped in sin—the adulterer, the addict, the cheater? Do you offer that person the love of Christ and His forgiveness? Or do you judge and condemn him?

We're all sinners, saved by grace. Can we do any less than Jesus did in offering compassion and forgiveness in place of accusation and condemnation?

Take a Look "So now there is no condemnation for those who belong to Christ Jesus" (Romans 8:1). Read the next three verses of Romans chapter 8. Why can't the law save anyone?

ALL TIED UP

 And he who had died came out bound hand and foot with graveclothes, and his face was wrapped with a cloth. Jesus said to them, "Loose him, and let him go." John 11:44 NKJV

MARY WAS HAVING an affair with a single man in her church. Mary's husband, Ted, confronted her and finally threatened to divorce her, but she continued to meet Ken. Ted met with their pastor and told him of the situation. The pastor called Mary in and she admitted that she was having a relationship with Ken. The pastor told her firmly that she had to stop, giving biblical support for why adultery is a sin. Mary agreed, tearfully apologized to Ted, and said she would stop seeing Ken.

The pastor referred Mary and Ted to a Christian counselor and also asked each of them to get involved with an accountability group of peers. If Mary and Ted could meet regularly with a group it could help them stay on track in implementing the changes that would be necessary to save their marriage. Both agreed to follow the pastor's advice.

Two months later, Ted learned that Mary had gone to dinner with Ken while Ted was on a business trip. He called the pastor, who tried to call Mary. She wouldn't return his calls. The pastor also called Ken, but he didn't call the pastor back either.

The pastor's numerous attempts to counsel Mary and Ken about their choice proved futile. Six months later Mary and Ken were still meeting and no action had been taken by the church since neither would meet with the pastor or elders or listen to their advice. Ted thought more should be done, but the pastor and elders explained that unless the couple was willing to submit their lives to Christ and repent of their sins, there was nothing more the church could do.

Mary and Ken were experiencing the spiritual death that

happens when we are cut off from the life of God because of sin. The Bible says "For the wages of sin is death" (Romans 6:23 NKJV), and "She who lives in pleasure is dead while she lives" (1 Timothy 5:6 NKJV).

Mary was "dead while she lives," and both her husband and her church had tried to intervene to help her return to the path of right living. But without her willingness to change, neither the church nor her husband could force her to break from her sin. They had tried to be involved in her restoration, as God calls believers to do, but the decision to end the relationship was ultimately hers.

When Jesus raised Lazarus from the dead, He asked the witnesses there to help free Lazarus from the death he had experienced. When Lazarus came out of the grave, he was wrapped like a mummy, bound by strips of cloth. He was no longer dead, but he was restricted. He couldn't do much all tied up.

But Jesus didn't take the graveclothes off of Lazarus Himself. He told the others present to turn him loose. That responsibility applies to the church, too—not only to call people forth to follow Jesus, but also to loose them and set them free.

This is a beautiful picture of our new life in Christ. We no longer live bound by the past, wearing the graveclothes of our old lives. We have been set free.

That is our challenge in the church: to help people live in freedom. Jesus told Lazarus's friends to loose him; it's our job to hold one another accountable, to confront sin when we see it—not in a judgmental, condemning sort of way, but in love. It's not that we should go around pointing fingers at one another; on the other hand, we can't turn a blind eye to ongoing sinful behavior and never mention it to the person.

Some Christians have come out of the grave, and while they're alive in Christ, they're still all wrapped up in the graveclothes of the past. They are bound by their old ways, appetites, and desires.

Once we are raised with Jesus, we should really live like

brand-new creatures, not all tied up with the past and the brokenness, death, and decay of sin. Jesus helps with the real problems we face, the temptations and sins that tie us up.

Paul told the Colossian church, "But now is the time to get rid of anger, rage, malicious behavior, slander, and dirty language. Don't lie to each other, for you have stripped off your old evil nature and all its wicked deeds. In its place you have clothed yourselves with a brand-new nature that is continually being renewed as you learn more and more about Christ, who created this new nature within you" (Colossians 3:8-10).

Church leadership, too, is responsible for dealing with evil. Church discipline is all about restoration, helping people live right and be free from the bondage of sin. If we don't address it in the church, the natural consequences will still occur, wreaking havoc in the lives of many.

If we can address sin with one another, repent, ask forgiveness, and move on, we'll be helping to loose the graveclothes of other believers and also of ourselves.

What about You? Are you willing to prayerfully get involved in speaking the truth in love to a fellow believer who is tied up in sin? Do you have a friend who needs help with accountability in handling a particular struggle?

On the other hand, is there an area of your life that you need to deal with as sin? Are you bound by graveclothes from your former life, your former ways and habits? Has a friend or loved one or someone in authority from your church talked to you about something in your life that is wrong? What was your response?

Ask God to give you boldness and gentleness with others and also with yourself, as you address difficult areas of struggle.

Take a Look Read 2 Corinthians 3:17-18 to learn how many of us are still in the process of being transformed into the likeness of Christ.

WINNING AT WORK

 Nevertheless even among the rulers many believed in Him, but because of the Pharisees they did not confess Him, lest they should be put out of the synagogue; for they loved the praise of men more than the praise of God. John 12:42-43 NKJV

CAN YOU LIVE the Christian life and still be successful in business or a career? The answer is absolutely yes. God put the desire to achieve into each of us, and hard work is good for us. In Ecclesiastes we read, "Nothing is better for a man than that he should eat and drink, and that his soul should enjoy good in his labor. This also, I saw, was from the hand of God" (Ecclesiastes 2:24 NKJV). Work is from the hand of God.

Many who are unemployed or too sick to work understand what a privilege work is. The ability to work, the opportunity to work, and the skills necessary to work are marvelous gifts. We sometimes groan at the thought of Monday morning rolling around again and drawing us back to work, but work is actually beneficial to us. Studies have shown that older individuals who continue to work or volunteer actively remain healthy longer and have less likelihood of getting Alzheimer's or other memory-related diseases.

Besides being a privilege, work is also a responsibility. The Bible says that each person should be productive: "For even when we were with you, we commanded you this: If anyone will not work, neither shall he eat" (2 Thessalonians 3:10 NKJV). And in 1 Timothy, Paul says, "If anyone does not provide for his own, and especially for those of his household, he has denied the faith and is worse than an unbeliever" (1 Timothy 5:8 NKJV).

Jesus Christ, the real God, worked as a carpenter. Even though He could have simply caused money to miraculously appear, He labored in a real occupation.

Work is a privilege; work is a responsibility; but work is not to be the preeminent focus of life, causing us to desire the praise of those in our industry, in the media, or among our colleagues, more than we want to please God.

Like most other good things, work can become an idol when it takes center stage in our thought life, our time and attention, and our reliance on it. What we love often occupies our thoughts.

So if work is good, but it can become bad, what's the answer? How do we handle work properly? First, we must define what true success is. It's not what we own, what we earn, or what we learn. Success is what we are and whether we are in the process of becoming the person God wants us to be. You can be rich or poor and be very successful; or you can be rich or poor and be a failure. It all depends on character and obedience to God— whether you're the same person in private as you are in public, whether you're genuine or fake.

Second, we must remember that work is not our ultimate priority and ask God to help us keep it in perspective. We should do our work with a standard of excellence and a strong work ethic, while keeping balance in our lives and remembering that even Jesus went off by Himself for refreshment. He told the disciples to "Come aside by yourselves to a deserted place and rest a while" (Mark 6:31 NKJV) when they were working among the crowds following Jesus.

And finally, we must be diligent to study the Bible and pray, asking God to keep our focus on Him and His purpose for us.

No matter what your work is—teacher, salesperson, executive, attorney, homemaker, caregiver, or police officer—you can succeed by appreciating your work, balancing your work and nonwork life, and obeying God at home as well as in the workplace.

What about You? Do you have your work life in balance? Do you work with diligence and energy in a way that will honor

SECTION 2: BREAKER OF MY CHAINS

God? Do you take appropriate weekend and vacation breaks for refreshment and renewal of relationships?

During the next week, make a note of the hours you work and the hours you rest, and see if you are spending appropriate time on each.

Take a Look In Galatians 6:7-10 find two results of doing good work.

BETRAYAL

When Jesus had said these things, He was troubled in spirit, and testified and said, "Most assuredly, I say to you, one of you will betray Me." Then the disciples looked at one another, perplexed about whom He spoke. . . . "It is he to whom I shall give a piece of bread when I have dipped it." And having dipped the bread, He gave it to Judas Iscariot, the son of Simon. Now after the piece of bread, Satan entered him.
John 13:21-22, 26-27 NKJV

THE CHEATING BUSINESS partner, the faithless spouse, the backstabbing friend—nothing hurts quite like betrayal.

When Harry learned that Len had run up staggering indebtedness for their insurance agency without Harry's knowledge, money that would take years to repay, Harry asked why. "You have to spend money to make money, Harry, and you just wouldn't do it." Len had been banking on future growth and income for the agency, growth that never materialized.

The day the business closed its doors for the last time, Len disappeared, leaving Harry responsible for all the debts of the partnership. The financial mess was overwhelming, but what hurt even more was the betrayal by a man Harry had trusted as a friend and business partner.

Jesus Christ knew all about betrayal. He knew all along what Judas would do, and yet He traveled with him in the group of disciples, treating him like all the others. We don't see Jesus berating Judas or shunning him, but rather loving His enemy, as He told us to do in Matthew 5:44. He even washed Judas's feet. Of course, He respected Judas's choices and allowed him to experience the consequences of his actions.

Often the appropriate way to love someone who mistreats us is to allow the person to experience the consequences of that wrongdoing, which may include losing the relationship. Much has been said about "tough love," and sometimes the loving thing to do is to stop allowing the wrong behavior to continue. The parent who again and again intercedes on behalf of his high-schooler who has ditched classes and failed tests may be helping or enabling the child to continue in his or her irresponsible and harmful behavior. The child is actually betraying himself and his future. The wife who forgives infidelity again and again, even when the promises to stop, are never kept allows her husband to continue betraying her and their family.

But praying for betrayers, showing kindness when appropriate, and speaking honestly and in love is always right.

Jesus experienced the pain of betrayal, yet He showed us, both by His actions and His words, how to handle it. And He will give us the strength to handle even a devastating life event like this and move beyond it.

What about You? Have you experienced betrayal by someone you trusted? Have you been able to get past it or does it still torment you today? Or have you been a betrayer? Is there someone you need to go to and confess, asking their forgiveness?

Jesus Christ understands betrayal better than anyone else. He was betrayed by a close friend and follower, and it led to His death. Ask Him to help you deal with the betrayals in your life and to heal and change you.

Take a Look Do you want to know the way to treat enemies? Read Luke 6:27-36.

A LEGACY OF PEACE

 Peace I leave with you, My peace I give to you; not as the world gives do I give to you. Let not your heart be troubled, neither let it be afraid. John 14:27 NKJV

PEACE is more than the absence of conflict, although in today's world, that sounds very appealing. How great it would be if there were peace in the world's trouble spots like the Middle East, Africa, and elsewhere.

But the peace Jesus talked about is more than an absence of conflict. His was a peace that remained when He came face-to-face with Satan, when the soldiers came to arrest Him in the garden of Gethsemane, and when He was falsely accused and condemned to die. It is an internal, invisible, and yet unmistakable peace—the peace of God. The apostle Paul called it, "the peace of God, which surpasses all understanding" (Philippians 4:7 NKJV).

Jesus promised to leave that marvelous peace with us, but it can be hard to experience it during difficult times.

Gwen and Rose shared a room at the nursing home. Both women were in their eighties, and both were widows. Gwen had Parkinson's disease, but she had lived in her own apartment until she fell and broke her leg. Unable to walk without assistance, Gwen's daughter, Gloria, had helped her mother settle into the room. After Gloria went home to be with her husband and son, Gwen said to Rose, "So this is what the golden years are all about. I just want to get out of here!" She pressed the red call button, and when the nurse appeared, Gwen said, "I need the curtains closed. There's too much light in here. And when can I leave? It smells in here."

Rose knew her residency in the nursing home was permanent. Her debilitating cancer caused her to be bedridden, and she was only able to sit up in a reclining chair for an hour or so twice a day. She still tried to read, but even that was becoming difficult. Yet Rose radiated a supernatural joy that elevated her above her dismal circumstances.

"Welcome to our room," she said to Gwen. "I have books and magazines if you'd like to do any reading."

Gwen snarled that she was going to get out of the place and didn't feel like reading.

"I'll pray that you heal quickly so you can leave," Rose said. "But once you're here a few days, you'll see that it's not so bad. The nurses are wonderful and kind, and their assistants take good care of us. Let me know if I can help you at all."

The presence of Jesus can provide true peace wherever we are. It's not passive indifference or detachment from reality. It's a deep abiding sense that in the grand scheme of things, God will make everything turn out right.

How can we attain this kind of peace? The first step is obedience to God's Word. Psalm 119:1-3 (NKJV) says, "Blessed are the undefiled in the way, who walk in the law of the LORD! Blessed are those who keep His testimonies, who seek Him with the whole heart! They also do no iniquity; they walk in His ways." Does this mean that obedient people never sin? No, but they try to obey what they know God wants them to do, and when they fail, they ask Him to forgive them and set them back on the right path.

The second way to experience peace is to focus on God's presence. Isaiah 26:3 (NKJV) says, "You will keep him in perfect peace, whose mind is stayed on You." Rose took her focus off herself and her illness and onto the needs of Gwen when she offered to pray for her. Memorizing and reciting Bible verses appropriate to your area of struggle can move your focus from your circumstances to God. As you learn verses that tell you not to worry or be anxious (such as Philippians 4:6-7), they will remind you that God wants you to trust Him with even the heaviest burdens.

The third step toward peace is putting your problem or situation into God's hands, realizing that He can handle it while you often cannot.

Jesus obeyed His Father; He knew the Word; and He submitted to God's will. He often went off alone to pray. And He experienced the amazing, genuine peace that He promised to leave behind for us, in all of our circumstances.

What about You? What will your legacy be? Do you leave behind peace or turmoil? Are you known more for worried hand-wringing or smiling serenity? Do others feel a calm in your presence, or is there a nervous, tense, or stressed atmosphere when you're around?

Jesus left peace behind for His disciples and for us today. Ask Him to calm you, to give you the peace that passes understanding in your daily life, so that you, too, can leave peace as your legacy.

Take a Look Look up Psalm 34:14 and Colossians 3:15. What two things can you do to experience more of God's peace?

WORK IN PROGRESS

 The world's sin is unbelief in me. Righteousness is available because I go to the Father, and you will see me no more.
John 16:9-10

HAVE YOU EVER had a personal trainer? That fit and trim taskmaster who tries to whip you into shape in the gym? The man or woman who is a combination of encourager, coach, and disciplinarian?

Your trainer wants you to be your physical best, to grow stronger, more agile, and healthier. That's why he works you so hard; he's on your side.

God's Spirit is the believer's very real Personal Trainer in the spiritual realm. He wants us to be like Jesus, possessing and demonstrating genuine righteousness, and He prods, pokes, and challenges us along the pathway toward spiritual fitness. He, too, is on our side.

A rather cumbersome theological word, *sanctification,* is the goal at the end of the pathway, and that word simply means becoming more like Christ, becoming holy. God said to Moses, "You must be holy because I, the LORD your God, am holy" (Leviticus 19:2).

Of course, we humans will never be truly holy as God is holy because we continue to struggle with our sinful nature all our lives. We will never be perfect like He is. But we can be in the process of becoming holy. We can be moving toward the goal.

Occasionally, we hear of a person who, upon conversion to Christ, immediately and permanently forsakes past addictions or habits. That doesn't mean she becomes sinless, but she is relieved of the intense craving she had experienced previously in a certain area. Most of us, even after we give our lives to Jesus, continue to experience the pull toward former behaviors.

We may resist the pull one day and fall into it the next. Life-long—or years long—patterns are usually not easily broken.

But we learn here that righteousness is available to us. Jesus, through His Spirit, gives us the power to say no to even the most stubborn sin. "He who has begun a good work in you will complete it until the day of Jesus Christ" (Philippians 1:6 NKJV). Our Personal Trainer is never going to give up on us, no matter how often we fail, no matter the horrible consequences we experience as a result of our sin. He will always tell us to get up and get going again because He will complete our training and deliver us to the goal.

What about You? What areas of your "training" are you working on right now? Are you following the instructions of God's Spirit as He guides and directs your fitness program, or do you sometimes turn a deaf ear to His whisperings when you want to "do your own thing" again?

Remember that our Trainer isn't just available on Tuesdays and Thursdays at 4 P.M. He's right here with us all the time, 24/7, ready to coax us along toward the genuine righteousness of Christ.

Take a Look Read Romans 4:16-22 and find out why Abraham was considered righteous even though he was a sinful human being just like the rest of us.

LIFE'S TOUGH CALLS

 Now there stood by the cross of Jesus His mother, and His mother's sister, Mary the wife of Clopas, and Mary Magdalene. When Jesus therefore saw His mother, and the disciple whom He loved standing by, He said to His mother, "Woman, behold your son!" Then He said to the disciple, "Behold your mother!" And from that hour that disciple took her to his own home. John 19:25-27 NKJV

ONE OF THE LAST things Jesus did before He died was to take care of His mother. From the cross, He asked John to provide for her once Jesus was gone, another example of the extreme love He demonstrated all His life. The book of John is the only Gospel account of these two statements in which Jesus fulfilled the commandment to honor one's parent.

At the time, women owned no property and had no income, so they had to be provided for by husbands, sons, or brothers. Jesus had brothers who would probably have taken care of Mary, but Jesus didn't want to leave this earth without putting her well-being into the hands of His beloved disciple John. Today caring for the elderly is considerably different. Women often have income and assets they can use for their care, and since many husbands and wives both work outside the home, it may be impossible to care for an elderly parent with dementia or Alzheimer's disease at home.

Pat and Jared wrestled with the decision as to what type of care would be best for Jared's mother, Alice. Alice had had two small strokes and was somewhat impaired in her ability to prepare meals and get up and down the stairs in her small home. Pat worked part-time as a salesperson, and she knew Alice would be home alone during those hours if she came to live with them. Alice's modest income would cover the major portion of nursing home care, and the sale of her home would cover the rest for some time. Pat's father had lived in a nursing home for the last fifteen months of his life because he had fallen several times and had also accidentally started a kitchen fire when he forgot about a pan of scrambled eggs on the stove. Although Pat had felt guilty about the decision she and her brothers had made, her father had been well cared for and safe during his last year. He seemed content in his surroundings during Pat's frequent visits, and she knew the nursing home had been the right decision.

While deciding about Alice's living arrangements, Pat and Jared heard advice on all sides of the issue, but they finally realized that either decision would be right. They loved Alice and showed their love regularly with visits, calls, and small gifts, all of which would continue no matter where she lived. Their decision to invite her to live in their home pleased Alice and resulted in months of good memories while she lived there.

Again and again, Jesus talked about and demonstrated real love, not about rules and guilt-inducing *must*s and *should*s. Sometimes a difficult decision can be made easier if we realize that there is freedom in true love, freedom to do what is best for all concerned, no matter what others may say.

What about You? Have you felt pressured by friends or acquaintances who tell you what you should do, even if it doesn't seem appropriate for you or your family?

As long as we are responsible and loving, creative solutions to problems can usually be found.

Take a Look In Isaiah 30:21, God said He will direct us when we ask for help with hard decisions. Make a note of this verse for the next time you need help with a decision.

BEHIND CLOSED DOORS

That evening, on the first day of the week, the disciples were meeting behind locked doors because they were afraid of the Jewish leaders. Suddenly, Jesus was standing there among them! "Peace be with you," he said. As he spoke, he held out his hands for them to see, and he showed them his side. They were filled with joy when they saw their Lord! He spoke to them again and said, "Peace be with you. As the Father has sent me, so I send you." John 20:19-21

THEY HAD DESERTED Him at His hour of agony. Except for John, the disciples had scattered after Jesus was arrested.

In John 20 they were undoubtedly dejected at their failure to stay with Jesus until the end as they met to ask each other, "Where do we go from here; what do we do next?" They feared the Jews would blame them for stealing Jesus' body. They knew He had risen, but they thought now they were on their own.

How like Jesus to come to His friends behind the locked doors, in spite of their failures. When we're locked up by the chains of sin, when we feel like failures, when we are in the midst of turmoil, He still comes to offer peace. Locks and chains can't keep Him out of our lives unless we let them, unless we give in to the paralysis that comes from self-doubt and defeat.

We wonder if Jesus was tempted to ask the disciples, "Where were you guys when I needed you?" Did He feel like expressing His disappointment and hurt at being abandoned at the hour of death?

Not Jesus. He came offering peace. He knew they would fail at times and He knew how they felt. But He also knew He had important work for them to do, work they couldn't do if they stayed locked behind closed doors nursing their wounds. They needed to go out and tell the world that He had risen, and He made that possible when He appeared to them here.

Dave had lived a locked-up life for four years, addicted to Internet porn. His wife had discovered his secret and confronted him. He wanted to stop, and he promised he would. But he used his computer in his work from his home office, and even his strongest determination faltered when the images popped up on his monitor.

His wife begged him to get counseling, and Dave finally talked to his pastor about the problem. The pastor agreed to hold Dave accountable with weekly reporting sessions. For six weeks, Dave was successful. He felt free, and he thanked the pastor for helping him with his problem.

But one night when he was working late he decided that since he had broken his habit he was now strong enough to be able to "just take a quick look." Dave cancelled his meeting with the pastor for that Saturday morning, and he never went back. He eventually lost his wife and two children in divorce.

Jesus is waiting to help Dave with his secret, to meet with him behind his closed doors and free him of his addiction. Instead of condemnation, He offers genuine peace and freedom to those who are struggling and guilty. He promises to make a way out to all who really want it (1 Corinthians 10:13).

What about You? What do you keep locked behind a closed door? Is there an area of your life you have kept God and others out of for fear of condemnation and rejection?

Jesus isn't squeamish about our bad habits, our evil thoughts, our repeated failures. He offered peace to His disciples who had deserted Him. He wants to put peace into your life as well.

Take a Look Read Mark 4:39 and Luke 4:35. Memorize one of these verses and recite it whenever you are worried that even Jesus can't provide the peace and freedom you need.

SECTION 3

King of My World

THE BIG PICTURE

 No one has ever seen God. But his only Son, who is himself God, is near to the Father's heart; he has told us about him. John 1:18

A SEMINARY PROFESSOR was well-known for how he taught his students the "observation" step in Bible study methods. Without explanation he would show a short film clip showing a bank robbery in progress. Then he would pass out a list of questions about the film: How many people? Males or females? What kind of getaway car? Time of day? How were they dressed? The students were amazed at what they didn't see!

The immediate application of the exercise was to show students how easy it is to read the Bible and miss many important details. But he made a larger point as well: Everyone focuses on different things, seeing things from a unique perspective.

The apostle John's perspective focuses on Jesus as the Son of God. You can't afford to miss this. The purpose is summarized toward the end of the book, "But these are written so that you may believe that Jesus is the Messiah, the Son of God, and that by believing in him you will have life" (John 20:31).

As in Jesus' own time, people today see Jesus in different ways and believe different things about Him. Perspectives vary. But by far the most compelling reason to believe in Jesus is because He has demonstrated that He is the Son of God. He was the only sinless person ever—fully God and fully man—and the only one qualified and willing to give His life to pay for our sins.

In contemporary culture, people are often valued for their looks, or their wealth, or their achievements. We don't have a physical description of Jesus in the Bible, but we can imagine that He looked like a typical Jewish man of His time. The prophet Isaiah tells us that the Messiah was not particularly attractive in physical appearance; he was ordinary. ("There was nothing beautiful or majestic about his appearance, nothing to attract us to him" Isaiah 53:2.) His beauty was in His presence, His grace, His goodness, not in His physical characteristics. A person who valued people because of their appearance would likely have missed Him because of a skewed perspective, looking for the superficial instead of the solid.

The Old Testament predicts the Messiah. But if you have never read the New Testament, you will only see part of the picture. If you don't learn that the Messiah was Jesus, your perspective will be off. It's not enough to believe in God. Even Satan and his demons believe in God and tremble in His presence. But just believing in God is to be lacking in perspective. It's just part of the picture. The picture is not complete until you also see Jesus, God's Son, who gave His life for you.

We can also have an unbalanced perspective about grace and truth. Some people see God only as the God of grace, an accepting God who doesn't condemn or judge anyone. Their perspective is lacking the truth of His righteousness and purity. Others view God as harsh, rigid, and legalistic, missing the perspective of His grace.

We need to step back and view the complete picture: a glorious composite of God's love depicted in His Son.

What about You? From what angle do you view Jesus? Do you see Him as harsh and rigid, watching for your every mistake? Or do you look to Him mostly to provide favors and answer your prayers? If so, you need to broaden your perspective. How?

Take a Look In Matthew 16:13-17 Jesus tells us exactly who He is, leaving no confusion. List several alternative views of who Jesus is and why they are incorrect according to this verse.

THE LIFE OF THE PARTY

 When the master of ceremonies tasted the water that was now wine, not knowing where it had come from (though, of course, the servants knew), he called the bridegroom over. "Usually a host serves the best wine first," he said. "Then, when everyone is full and doesn't care, he brings out the less expensive wines. But you have kept the best until now!" This miraculous sign at Cana in Galilee was Jesus' first display of his glory. And his disciples believed in him. John 2:9-11

JUDY GARLAND WAS a Hollywood star best known as the youthful Dorothy in *The Wizard of Oz*. For many, a life of stardom seems like the ticket to success and fulfillment. And yet, near the end of her life, Judy Garland could no longer feel the magic of Dorothy's ruby red slippers. She wrote, "If I'm such a legend, why am I so lonely?"

Judy discovered what the bride and groom in Cana discovered, that disappointment is often the uninvited guest in life. Just as the wine ran out at the wedding, we also run out of things or people we need and want. Judy Garland ran out of people; she was lonely. Some people run out of money. Others run out of health. Still others run out of companionship or even the will to live.

But Jesus saved the day at the wedding and He can save you as well. He can provide what we need because He is Lord over everything. He owns it all and controls it all. And He promises to give us what we need.

The occasion of the wedding at Cana was the first time Jesus demonstrated that He was Lord of all. Just as He was born in a humble stable, He chose the wedding of an ordinary, nameless couple in a small town for the occasion of His first miracle.

When the wine supply ran out, Jesus had compassion for the host's feelings and His mother's desires. Using human instruments for the task, He told the servants to fill six large, empty water jars with water. He then transformed the water into the best wine the banquet steward had ever tasted—better than the wine the bridegroom had provided for the wedding. The steward thought his host was just being generous: the longer the party, the better the wine!

Think of what would have happened at the wedding had Jesus not been there. In that culture, the groom would have been ashamed because he ran out of wine. The guests would have become disgruntled, perhaps even leaving the party. What began as a celebration could have ended in catastrophe.

Jesus made the difference in the entire event. And He makes the difference in our lives as well. Without Him, we, too, have an empty life—empty of genuine joy. Apart from God, all the things we use to try to fill our lives will always run out and fail to satisfy, just as Judy Garland discovered. He alone can take our emptiness and transform it into something new and better than it was before.

But besides saving the wedding host from embarrassment, and besides displaying His power to do miracles, Jesus also demonstrated for the wedding guests, especially His disciples, several important principles.

First, the joy of a wedding feast is no insignificant matter to God. Jesus is Lord over all of life's celebrations, and He rejoices right along with us, just as He grieves with us over our losses. He genuinely shares in our victories and defeats because He loves and understands us.

Second, our best human efforts at making life meaningful will always fall short of God's plan to give our lives true meaning. As Lord over life, He fills our life with new wine. He shows us again and again that the best is yet to come, whether in this life or in the future in heaven. He saves the best until last, and as we get older, Jesus adds life to our years. Even as the body fails, our inner man (the real person) is renewed day by day (2 Corinthians 4:16).

And third, miracles are intended to reveal the glory of God (John 9:3). Jesus took everyday people and common events and used them to show God's power and glory. He is here for us in the everyday as well, revealing His glory, often in unexpected— and very real—ways.

What about You? Do you ever feel as though life has bottomed out? When you think of the best being yet to come, do you shake your head in doubt because of difficult experiences you have gone through? You may feel emotionally numb or empty because of disappointments or struggles or tragedies in your life. But Jesus Christ, compassionate Savior, can give your life new meaning. He longs to rejoice and cry with you, to show you that for you, too, the best is yet to come. He surprised the wine steward by giving the best as the last. Give Him that area of your life that you've almost given up on and watch Him handle it for you.

Take a Look Read Job 42:1-5 (NIV). Even after his tragic losses, Job said that through disaster God had shown him "things too wonderful for me to know." God had shown Himself to Job through it all: "My ears had heard of you but now my eyes have seen you."

Recall a time you saw God working in your life in the midst of trouble.

IF ONLY YOU HAD TOLD ME

 Do you think the work of harvesting will not begin until the summer ends four months from now? Look around you! Vast fields are ripening all around us and are ready now for the harvest. John 4:35

BASKETBALL GREAT Pete Maravich became a Christian after trying everything from New Age religion to Eastern mysticism. But once he came to faith in Christ, his life and his priorities changed. He said, "If I have the opportunity to choose the subject of the conversation, the subject is always going to be Jesus Christ."

The woman at the well shared Pete's conviction. Leaving her water jar—the reason she had come to the well—she ran into town, excited with her news: She had met the Christ! Hers was an extraordinarily successful missionary campaign—the entire town came out to meet Jesus because of what she said, and many believed.

What had been important to her just minutes before lost its urgency as the truth of her message drove her to share it with others, others who may have scorned her because of her reputation. None of that mattered; she had to tell of her experience with Jesus.

When Jesus met this woman, He demonstrated four characteristics of those who have become actual players instead of mere spectators in the harvest fields of the world. And in turn, the woman at the well also exhibited these characteristics when she ran to tell the townspeople.

First, Jesus was available. Available people have compassion for others. Jesus went into Samaria, a place Jews normally avoided. He knew there were people in Samaria who needed the gospel, so that's where He went. Available people go where there are people who need to hear.

Second, Jesus was authentic. Even though Jesus was the Messiah of Israel, He was not pretentious. He didn't lord it over the woman. He spoke truthfully and openly to her, simply telling her who she was and who He was. He was a genuine person giving a genuine witness of the truth about God. She in turn carried her own simple truth into town.

Third, Jesus loved unconditionally. The woman at the well had a stained past, as we all do in one way or another. She had had five husbands and was apparently living with a man to whom she wasn't married. Jesus wasn't offended by her past because He loved her unconditionally. She demonstrated this same love to the townspeople when she faced the prejudice undoubtedly aimed against her and relayed her news anyway.

Finally, Jesus presented the Good News urgently. He knew that there was no time like the present for this woman to believe. He invited her to drink of the living water and never thirst again (John 4:10). In turn, she conveyed urgency as she raced into town.

Talking about subjects with real significance can be hard, but it's absolutely necessary if we hope to make a difference.

What about You? When was the last time you talked to someone about Jesus? While the reward of helping someone find faith in Jesus is great, it can be scary until we realize that it's really not our responsibility to save anyone. Jesus will do the saving. Our job is simply to tell others what He means to us and what He's done in our lives—to say, "If you only knew Jesus . . ."

Jesus invited the woman at the well to Himself. He spoke honestly and directly to her, and she came. When she went to the city she found that the people were ready and responsive, and they came to Jesus, too. All she did was to share what she had experienced. He did the rest. And that's all we need to do.

SECTION 3: KING OF MY WORLD

Take a Look In Mark 16:15, Jesus said, "Go into all the world and preach the Good News to everyone, everywhere." Make a note of two places where you might find the opportunity to share Christ during the next week.

FOREVER—A LONG, LONG TIME

 The Father has life in himself, and he has granted his Son to have life in himself. And he has given him authority to judge all mankind because he is the Son of Man. Don't be so surprised! Indeed, the time is coming when all the dead in their graves will hear the voice of God's Son, and they will rise again. Those who have done good will rise to eternal life, and those who have continued in evil will rise to judgment.
John 5:26-29

SIR WILLIAM RUSSELL, the English patriot, was executed in 1683. As the time drew near, he took his watch out of his pocket, handed it to his attending physician, and said, "Would you kindly take my timepiece? I have no use for it now. I am dealing with eternity."

Each of us must deal with the reality of eternity, the great forever with no end. Every person—both believers and nonbelievers—will one day stand before God. What will that day be like?

While we will one day be immortal, we know we are not indestructible. Our bodies wear out, and we will die. The Bible encourages us to prepare in advance for death, for the day we will stand before God. We are to prepare by committing our lives to Christ and accepting His gift of eternal life. Because of what Jesus did for us, we can one day stand before God forgiven and welcomed.

There are many views on death and what happens after death, but the only authority on the subject is the Word of God, which describes judgment very clearly. Paul said in 2 Corinthians 5:10, "For we must all appear before the judgment seat of Christ" (NIV). The purpose of the judgment for believers is not condemnation because there is no condemnation for those who are in Christ. Nor is it a matter of deciding whether or not we will go to heaven. Jesus purchased that for us, once and for all.

111

The purpose of this judgment is to give an account of our lives and be evaluated for the rewards we will receive.

Unbelievers will face the Great White Throne Judgment described in Revelation 20:11-15. It will be a fearful time for those who have refused God's gift of salvation and must stand before Him to answer for their sins—sins Jesus Christ willingly died to pay for. Pride, arrogance, and ego will have been blown away, and every wrong will be made right.

Jesus Christ will be the Judge on that day, as we see in Acts: "He [Jesus] who was ordained by God to be Judge of the living and the dead" (Acts 10:42 NKJV). He is uniquely qualified to judge because He knows the human heart; He fully understands the motives behind our actions. We can count on His judgment being eminently fair, even for those who refuse His gift of eternal life purchased on the cross. So since we all sin, we all must choose. Your choice will determine whether your sin will be pardoned because of what Jesus did on the cross, or your sin will be punished in hell. The question is this: Will you receive the gift of forgiveness or reject it and be separated from God forever?

Yes, the topic of judgment is clear, although God wants none to be lost. He gave His Son so that anyone who believes will be spared the judgment of unbelievers. Unfortunately for those who think there are many routes to God, the Bible says that the one way to God is through Jesus Christ. It won't be good enough to say, "I was doing the best I could" or "I lived up to the standard of my religion, and I thought all roads lead to heaven."

Heaven and hell do exist. Every person will ultimately wind up in one place or the other. Thankfully, the simple gospel message makes heaven possible for all.

What about You? Will you stand before God forgiven because you have believed in Jesus as your Savior? Will you review your life with God as a forgiven saint? Or will you face the judgment of the unbeliever when it's too late to place your faith in Christ?

Make sure today that you are prepared to meet God. It could happen fifty years from now, or it could happen today. Be ready.

Take a Look In Malachi 4:1-2 we read, "The LORD Almighty says, 'The day of judgment is coming, burning like a furnace. The arrogant and the wicked will be burned up like straw on that day. They will be consumed like a tree—roots and all. But for you who fear my name, the Sun of Righteousness will rise with healing in his wings. And you will go free, leaping with joy like calves let out to pasture.'"

Read more about rejoicing at the time of judgment in Revelation 19:1-5.

THE EYES HAVE IT

 If I bear witness of Myself, My witness is not true. There is another who bears witness of Me, and I know that the witness which He witnesses of Me is true. You have sent to John, and he has borne witness to the truth. Yet I do not receive testimony from man, but I say these things that you may be saved. He was the burning and shining lamp, and you were willing for a time to rejoice in his light. John 5:31-35 NKJV

MIKE STOOD BEFORE the judge and trembled. Sure, he had been at the crime scene. He was looking for his little brother, and he thought he saw him at the corner. Mike had parked his car and jumped out, hoping to persuade fourteen-year-old Frankie to come home, to get away from the corner crowd who were known for fighting and drugs.

Mike had just realized it wasn't Frankie after all when the first shot rang out. The others at the street corner scattered, leaving Mike paralyzed as he saw a teenage boy lying in a pool of blood. He was the only one there when the police arrived.

Fortunately for Mike, a witness on the third floor of a nearby apartment building had seen the whole episode. The woman had seen the boy with the gun crouch down and fire the weapon, had seen him run away and toss the gun into the dumpster, and she was willing to state what she had seen. Otherwise, Mike could well have wound up in prison.

Witnesses are very important. Jesus explained their importance in John 5 when He talked about those who were witnesses for Him.

John the Baptist was the first servant of God who testified as to who Jesus was. Crowds flocked to hear John's powerful preaching, but many fled when he hit the hard subjects such as righteousness, hypocrisy, and repentance. John's blunt talk to Herod led to his death. Today, people are eager to hear messages on success and health. But when topics like the need for repentance and living out faith in righteousness come up, they'd rather not listen. Jesus says in John 5:31-36 that not only is John a credible witness, but God Himself testifies as to who Jesus is. "And the Father Himself, who sent Me, has testified of Me. You have neither heard His voice at any time, nor seen His form" (John 5:37 NKJV). This was a courageous statement because He was talking to the learned religious leaders who prided themselves on their knowledge of God and claimed to speak for Him. Yet Jesus said they didn't know Him at all.

The disciples were witnesses for Jesus as well. After Jesus' death, they scattered around the world telling others about Him, and they were ultimately killed for their faith, as John had been. Had Jesus' identity and resurrection been a lie, surely the disciples would have recanted to save their lives.

We, too, are witnesses of who Jesus is. We have spiritual experience with Him because His Spirit lives in us. When Jesus answers a prayer, or shows you His power, you become a witness for Him, just as John and the disciples were. While our experiences with God are subjective, they're nevertheless valid and valuable to share with others.

What about You? Are you a burning and shining lamp for Jesus? Do you radiate light and joy and hope? Or are you full of complaints and gloom and darkness? If we hope to attract others to Jesus, the Light of the World who lives in each believer, we need to show others that knowing Him makes a difference in our lives, the difference between life and death, joy and despair, light and darkness.

Take a Look Read 1 John 5:9-10. Whose witness about Jesus is the greatest?

FROM HEAD TO HEART

 You search the Scriptures, for in them you think you have eternal life; and these are they which testify of Me. But you are not willing to come to Me that you may have life. I do not receive honor from men. But I know you, that you do not have the love of God in you. I have come in My Father's name, and you do not receive Me; if another comes in his own name, him you will receive. John 5:39-43 NKJV

STEPHEN WAS a second-year student at a prestigious law school. He planned to become a defense attorney and had modeled his career after Ira Walton, a well-known defense lawyer in his community. Stephen didn't approve of all of the lawyer's dealings or behavior, but he appreciated the attorney's ability to cross-examine witnesses. He practiced the man's techniques and studied his methods.

During one class session, Stephen found himself arguing with an older student who sat in the back of the large auditorium. The student was wearing sunglasses and a baseball cap and Stephen didn't know the student or recall seeing him before. As they talked, Stephen vehemently decried his position on the way a hypothetical trial should be handled, frequently quoting Ira Walton to back up his claims.

At the end of the class, the professor introduced the older "student" as Ira Walton, the famous role model Stephen longed to emulate in his career. The defense attorney commended Stephen's grasp of his trial techniques, but said he had missed the point that a defense lawyer needs to understand the motivation of his witness above all. More than technique or strategy, the lawyer needs to know what's important to the person. He said Stephen had acquired knowledge, but not understanding.

People can acquire knowledge of the Bible while lacking understanding. The Bible is sometimes studied as great literature, allegory, myth, or fiction. A movie called *The Greatest Story Ever Told* even features Bible characters and events. There are scholars today who study the Bible as an intellectual pursuit. But Jesus pointed out to the Jewish leaders that reading the Scriptures, knowing the stories, and keeping the rules are not enough. He said it is possible to know the Word of God without knowing the God of the Word.

The Pharisees knew the Old Testament Scriptures from cover to cover. They knew Moses and the patriarchs and the prophets. They revered Moses who predicted the coming of Jesus. Jesus said, "For if you believed Moses, you would believe Me; for he wrote about Me" (John 5:46 NKJV). Although Jesus explained the Old Testament symbols, prophecies, and laws that concerned Him, the Pharisees still didn't recognize Him as the promised Messiah.

All their knowledge and all the evidence did not convince them to believe in Christ. Their hearts were hard and without love, showing no evidence of a genuine relationship with God. It was almost as though their knowledge and their good deeds stood in the way of them placing simple, childlike faith in Christ. Their knowledge puffed them up and made them think they were superior. It blinded them from seeing the Messiah when He stood right in front of them. They thought they had God all figured out intellectually, but they didn't take that all-important step of testing Him and trying Him and trusting Him. They wouldn't try Him for themselves.

I love chocolate pie. In fact, there are only two kinds of pie I like—hot pie and cold pie. But if I were describing chocolate pie to you and you've never tasted it, I'd just have to tell you to try it for yourself.

Psalm 34:8 says, "Taste and see that the LORD is good. Oh, the joys of those who trust in him!" Experience the real God for yourself by putting your life—your entire life—into His hands.

What about You? Have you gone beyond intellectual knowledge of the Bible? You may be a Bible scholar or a seminary student, or a Bible teacher or a pastor. But have you taken the crucial step of trusting and trying Jesus, of seeing for yourself whether He is who He claims to be? You won't know unless you place your faith in Him and ask Him to reveal Himself to you. You can know about Him, but you can't know Him unless you try Him for yourself.

Take a Look Proverbs 1:7 (NKJV) says, "The fear of the LORD is the beginning of knowledge, but fools despise wisdom and instruction." Read Proverbs 2 and write down five benefits of wisdom.

WHEN LITTLE IS MUCH

 Another of his disciples, Andrew, Simon Peter's brother, spoke up, "Here is a boy with five small barley loaves and two small fish, but how far will they go among so many?" Jesus said, "Have the people sit down." There was plenty of grass in that place, and the men sat down, about five thousand of them. Jesus then took the loaves, gave thanks, and distributed to those who were seated as much as they wanted. He did the same with the fish. John 6:8-11 (NIV)

ONE HALLOWEEN when I was a child, we had forgotten to buy candy for the kids, so my dad scouted around the house for something to give the trick-or-treaters. He found some crackers and canned sardines, and this is what he passed out to the kids when they came to the door. They definitely got more of a trick than a treat at our house that year!

But sardines are much more like what the little boy in John 6 had than a large fish like a bass or trout. All he had was what his mother had packed him for lunch that morning. The five loaves were actually small, coarse barley loaves, like crackers or little biscuits. The fish were tiny, and the custom was to make a pickled relish out of small, sardine-size fish to spread on this little bread. This was a very tiny lunch that Andrew spotted in the crowd.

This miracle is the only one included in all four of the Gospels. It must be worthy of special notice. Of course, we don't know how Jesus did it, but He took the food in His hands and created more and more and more until there was plenty for all, plus leftovers. He took what was available, He thanked God for it, and He multiplied it.

What we give to Him, He takes, multiplies, and uses. The little boy gave everything he had, small though his lunch was. But that didn't limit God at all. He is able to take little resources and little people and use them as mightily as if they were large. No one is too small, insignificant, or incapable for God to use. He took a shepherd's rod, put it in the hand of Moses, and delivered a nation. He took a few small stones and a slingshot and won a great victory for his people through David. Little is much in the hands of God.

But we also see in these verses that in order to receive the food He would provide, the crowd needed to obey Him and sit down. They did exactly what He had said to do, and then they waited and watched to see Him work. The people counted on Him to provide, and He did. After the bread and fish lunch, everyone was full and there were twelve basketfuls left over.

Trust and obey sounds so simple, doesn't it? Yet that is exactly how we show that our faith is real—when we do what God asks and wait to see Him take care of us. When we exercise the power of trust, our lives are transformed as we see what He can do with what we've given Him to work with.

What about You? Have you put your resources—regardless of how limited or how extensive they are—into God's hands? Don't wait until you think you have enough or you're in the right position or situation to begin to turn your life and your possessions and your loved ones over to God to use. Do it today and watch Him transform your situation, your finances, and your family.

Take a Look "Now to Him who is able to do exceedingly abundantly above all that we ask or think, according to the power that works in us, to Him be glory in the church by Christ Jesus to all generations, forever and ever. Amen" (Ephesians 3:20-21 NKJV).

Make note of at least one time when God provided "exceedingly abundantly" for you.

THE CHOSEN

Then he said, "That is what I meant when I said that people can't come to me unless the Father brings them to me." At this point many of his disciples turned away and deserted him. Then Jesus turned to the Twelve and asked, "Are you going to leave, too?" Simon Peter replied, "Lord, to whom would we go? You alone have the words that give eternal life. We believe them, and we know you are the Holy One of God."
John 6:65-69

AS LONG AS HE COULD remember, Ben knew that he was adopted. His parents explained how they had longed for a child and how thrilled they had been when they got the opportunity to take Ben into their family. They described the way they had pursued Ben's adoption, filling out forms, being interviewed, meeting his birth mom, and praying that they would be chosen to be Ben's parents. They told him about the wonderful day he was born and their joy at bringing him home from the hospital.

All his life he knew he was wanted and chosen by his parents, who had made a special point of finding him and bringing him into their lives.

Jesus told us that we, too, have been chosen and pursued by God, who wanted to bring us into His family. He said no one would follow Him unless drawn by the Spirit of God who is at work behind the scenes in human destiny. Some people are troubled by this teaching of Jesus, asking, "Are you saying that God and God alone chooses people for salvation and only the people God chooses will go to heaven?" That's exactly what Jesus said in this verse. They respond, "But don't we have a will, a choice?" The Bible teaches that we do have a choice. We choose to come to Christ, but we come because God calls us.

Jesus died for the whole world, and God doesn't want anyone to be lost. "He does not want anyone to perish, so he is giving more time for everyone to repent" (2 Peter 3:9). But He has chosen us before the foundation of the world (Ephesians 1:4). Before I was ever born, God chose me.

The great British preacher Charles Spurgeon said, "It's a good thing God chose us before we were born, else He probably wouldn't have done it after we were born."

The big question is: How can you know if you're chosen or not? The answer is simple: You can put your faith in Christ, and that means you're chosen because only God's Spirit can enable you to do that. It's as if you were walking down a road and came to a door on which is posted an invitation to eternal life and happiness. You've seen other people going in the door. You stop and think and then by faith you turn the doorknob, open the door, and walk in. The door closes behind you and you look at the other side of the door with these inscribed words: "You didn't choose Me, I chose you." There's the earthly side of our perspective, how we see the choice to come to Christ; and also the divine side, how God sees it. Jesus tells us, "All that the Father gives Me will come to Me, and the one who comes to Me I will by no means cast out" (John 6:37 NKJV).

It's a legitimate choice. We can either accept or refuse God's love extended to all of us.

What about You? Have you turned the doorknob and entered the door to eternal life with Christ? Or are you bothered that only God chooses who will enter? Does the seeming unfairness and exclusivity of this fact keep you out of God's family?

God invites you to come on in. Once you enter that door, you will know that you made a good choice. You will know that you have found the Holy One of God who alone can offer eternal life.

Take a Look Read Isaiah 43:1-4. List three specific benefits of being called or chosen by God found in these verses.

FINDING FAULT

 As Jesus was walking along, he saw a man who had been blind from birth. "Teacher," his disciples asked him, "why was this man born blind? Was it a result of his own sins or those of his parents?" "It was not because of his sins or his parents' sins," Jesus answered. "He was born blind so the power of God could be seen in him." John 9:1-3

WHEN TED WAS stricken with Parkinson's disease, a church elder suggested he search his conscience for the sin that had led to his condition. Ted was flabbergasted by this idea—flabbergasted and badly hurt.

"I know I'm not perfect, but I really don't think this is the result of my sin," he said.

"It's definitely a possibility because we reap what we sow," the elder stated firmly.

This church officer was twisting biblical principles in an abusive way, and he was speaking in direct contradiction to Jesus' own words.

In John 9:1-3 Jesus was leaving the Temple after a confrontation with the religious leaders in Jerusalem who wanted to stone Him for His claims. Yet He noticed this blind man and stopped to help him. His genuine love was greater than His desire to get away from His accusers. In healing the man's blindness, Jesus freed him from physical darkness. But in stating that the blindness was not his fault or his parents' fault, He also freed him from guilt and shame. In His pure love for the man, He addressed the totality of his needs. Not only did He meet the man's need for physical sight but He also provided emotional release of the burden he had no doubt carried all his life. Common teaching of that day said that either he or his parents were at fault for his blindness.

In Jesus' time, both the Greeks and the Jews assumed that all suffering was a direct result of sin. Some rabbis taught "prenatal sin," pointing to how Jacob and Esau fought within the womb as proof of their erroneous idea that a baby can actually sin before birth. They also taught that children paid for their parents' sin, citing Exodus 34:7 (NKJV): "Visiting the iniquity of the fathers upon the children and the children's children to the third and the fourth generation."

Children can suffer the consequences of their parents' sin, as when the child of an addict is born addicted. And harmful family behavioral and relational patterns can be passed down because parents have significant influence on their children. But ultimately, each person is responsible for his own sin. Parents have a heavy responsibility to do right by their children, but there is no curse passed down from generation to generation.

To be sure, sinful choices do sometimes lead to health consequences, as when a person drives drunk and gets in an automobile accident. But Jesus makes it perfectly clear that illness or disability often has absolutely nothing to do with the sins of the sick person.

Sickness can be an authentic platform for the display of God's power, as it was here. God's power can be seen in sickness, whether or not God miraculously heals the individual, as Jesus did with the man born blind. But God often gives ill people the supernatural ability to bear their pain with grace, and that, too, displays His power. He gives them an unfathomable but real peace in the midst of their suffering.

So if it's not because of the man's sin or his parents' sin, why was he born blind? Jesus said it was for a higher purpose in his life and in the lives of others. The higher purpose is that God's power was proven through the man's faith and his healing.

What about You? Have you been wondering for years what you did wrong that made you suffer as you have in some area of your life? Have you felt shame and guilt because of a problem you have that was not the result of your actions or behavior?

Take it to Jesus right now and ask Him to bring glory to God through your problem and the way you handle it. Ask Him to take the shame and guilt you have carried around because you assumed that it's all your fault.

Take a Look Read Joel 2:26-27 and Romans 9:33. What can you conclude about God and shame?

FOR SURE AND CERTAIN

 And I give them eternal life, and they shall never perish; neither shall anyone snatch them out of My hand. My Father, who has given them to Me, is greater than all; and no one is able to snatch them out of My Father's hand.
John 10:28-29 NKJV

STEVE AND BECKY'S nineteen-year-old son Brian was in court—again. This was his second ticket for driving while under the influence of alcohol. Last year he had been arrested for possession of marijuana for which he was fined and required to do twenty hours of community service. His parents had tried to convince him to get counseling or to attend an Alcoholics Anonymous meeting, but Brian insisted he didn't have a problem. "Everyone does it occasionally, and I just happened to get caught," he said. Steve and Becky insisted that he pay the fines himself, and they refused to hire a lawyer to try to reduce or eliminate the penalty for his latest problem.

They loved their son deeply, but they knew they needed to hold Brian responsible for his actions. They stood by, ready to help if he was ready to face the truth, but they refused to participate in any way that could enable him to continue in his harmful behavior.

Even though Brian's parents chose to love their wayward son from a distance, they didn't expel him from the family or cease to love him. The family tie was a permanent one.

In the same way, as Christians, we can be sure that our family relationship to God is real and permanent. He will never kick us out of the family, although He will allow us to experience the painful consequences of our choice to sin. But once we are His, we are His forever.

Jesus stated it twice in John 10:28-29: Our salvation is secure and permanent. Many places in the Bible support this foundational statement. In Romans we read, "For God's gifts and his call can never be withdrawn" (Romans 11:29). And in 1 Corinthians 1:8 (NKJV), we see the same idea: "[Jesus Christ] will also confirm you to the end, that you may be blameless in the day of our Lord Jesus Christ."

Our security is based on the Word of our heavenly Father and His faithfulness. "He who has begun a good work in you will complete it until the day of Jesus Christ" (Philippians 1:6 NKJV). God is committed to our spiritual success and our eternal salvation, and His commitment can't be undone. Nor can the finished work of Christ on the cross be undone. When He said, "It is finished," in John 19:30, He completed the work of saving us once and for all.

To be sure, sin separates us from God, grieves God, and brings disaster into our lives, but it doesn't remove us from God's family. His faithfulness and Christ's completed work on the cross prevent that.

But what about those who profess faith, attend church, serve in church, and then drop out and turn their backs on God? Do those people lose their salvation?

Many of those who fall away never were really a part of the family, and this occurred even among Jesus' own disciples. Although Judas would betray Jesus, the disciples thought he was a good guy, even appointing him treasurer of the group. He looked and talked and acted like a believer, but he had never truly repented and given his life to Jesus Christ.

This kind of person is described in 1 John 2:19 (NLT): "These people left our churches because they never really belonged with us; otherwise they would have stayed with us. When they left us, it proved that they do not belong with us."

There are also genuine believers who fall away from walking with Jesus. But in their case, just as Steve and Becky remained Brian's parents and longed for him to return to right living, God allows us to stray if we want to; He allows us to experience the results of sin; and He pursues us until we finally realize, with the Prodigal Son, that the only place we're at home is with the Father.

How can you know for sure if you are a true believer? He is faithful to save you if you confess your sins and ask Jesus Christ to forgive you and then you turn away from your past life to try to follow Him as best you can. He will supplant your old desires with new and better ones. That is not to say that you won't be tempted by old ways, but Jesus will slowly, inexorably, change your life. A true believer's life will bear fruit—not necessarily in the form of a showy public ministry or in dozens of people being led to Christ, but in countless small ways as we live in obedience to the Bible day in and day out.

What about You? Have you made a genuine commitment to Christ? Does your life bear some fruit in the form of love toward others and obedience to the truths you know? Or do you talk and act and look like a Christian on the outside without ever having made that life-changing commitment?

Go to God today, without reservation, and ask Him to take control of your life. His faithfulness and Christ's finished work on the cross are all you need for a fruitful life now and eternal life later.

Take a Look Read Romans 8:38-39 to learn more about our certainty that nothing can separate us from God's love.

GIVERS AND TAKERS

Then Mary took a pound of very costly oil of spikenard, anointed the feet of Jesus, and wiped His feet with her hair. And the house was filled with the fragrance of the oil. But one of His disciples, Judas Iscariot, Simon's son, who would betray Him, said, "Why was this fragrant oil not sold for three hundred denarii and given to the poor?" This he said, not that he cared for the poor, but because he was a thief, and had the money box; and he used to take what was put in it. But Jesus said, "Let her alone; she has kept this for the day of My burial. For the poor you have with you always, but Me you do not have always." John 12:3-8 NKJV

JONATHAN FELT PLEASED when he was able to add his five thousand dollar check to the offering basket on Sunday. *I'm glad I closed that deal and can give this to our church,* he thought. *Yep, it feels good to be generous.* Jonathan's cut in the transaction he had completed three days before was nearly one hundred thousand dollars, but he was annoyed that his plant foreman had chosen this week to ask for a raise. *I could enjoy this windfall a lot more if I hadn't had to turn Bob down. But if I give him a raise, I'll have to increase the others' salaries, and before I know it, my profit on the deal will be evaporated.*

Bob, too, enjoyed being generous, even though sometimes it was hard to do financially. His modest salary didn't quite stretch far enough to cover his son's college tuition and the normal living expenses for his two high-school-age kids. Bob's wife worked, too, but it seemed as though there was always a budget shortage.

Bob was disappointed that Jonathan had turned down his request for an annual raise citing economic conditions within the industry. But he didn't regret offering to pay for his uninsured neighbor to go to the doctor about his lingering cough.

I can cut back somewhere else; Amos really needs some medical attention, Bob thought.

Jonathan and Bob are good examples of the difference between givers and takers. The book of John provides two more examples in Mary and Judas.

Mary was the introspective sister. While Martha bustled around the house getting ready for company, Mary sat at the feet of Jesus, listening and reflecting on His goodness to her. She wondered, *How can I show my love for the Lord Jesus?* She remembered a flask of precious ointment tucked away, perhaps in her hope chest for the day she would marry. She found the ointment, broke the seal, and poured it lovingly on His feet and wiped them with her hair. She gave the most valuable thing she owned to show her love for Him.

And while Judas criticized her for it, Jesus praised her, just as He praised the poor widow who gave her two small coins in Mark 12:42. These women gave all they had to show their love for God. The genuine Jesus spotted genuine generosity when He saw it.

Judas, on the other hand, tried to sound as though he cared for the poor while he was helping himself to the group treasury to which he had been entrusted. His critical, selfish spirit contrasted starkly with Mary's joyful and lavish giving.

A week later when the women went to the tomb to anoint Jesus' body for burial, they found they were too late because He was already gone. How fortunate that Mary had been listening at Jesus' feet, sensed that He was on His way to die, and anointed Him with her most valuable possession. She had been a genuine giver, even when criticized by a taker.

What about You? Are you a giver or a taker? Or are you somewhere in between like most of us? What concrete steps can you take today to move further along the continuum from being a taker to being a giver? What need do you know of that you can meet, even if it means sacrificing your own plans or desires to do so?

Someone said that takers may eat better, but givers sleep better. Remember Jesus' affirming words about Mary's extravagant gift to Him. What He did for us was extravagant; our most magnanimous generosity could never approach the giving of Christ, but it could make Him smile.

Take a Look Read 2 Corinthians 8:1-5. What two things did the churches in Macedonia have that allowed them to overflow in rich generosity?

HOW DO YOU WORSHIP?

 The next day a great multitude that had come to the feast, when they heard that Jesus was coming to Jerusalem, took branches of palm trees and went out to meet Him, and cried out: "Hosanna! 'Blessed is He who comes in the name of the LORD*!' The King of Israel!"* John 12:12-13 NKJV

DISAGREEMENTS about worship styles have caused untold problems in churches. Some people like staid, traditional music; others prefer a lively, contemporary service. Some like organ music; others favor guitars and drums. In some churches worshipers are physically demonstrative, raising their hands, clapping, and swaying or dancing; in others, everyone stands still, arms at their sides.

Which type of worship is the right type? In John 12, we learn that it's not the form of worship that counts to God; it's the heart of the worshiper that is all-important. From our hearts come the visible expressions of our worship. It can include singing songs, praying, silent and audible worship, and giving, but worship is praising God for who He is, the genuine God, no matter what form that takes.

The crowd's energy and excitement are evident in these verses. No quiet, calm worship for these folks. They rushed to meet Him, palm branches waving, and crying out in worship.

Worship can be planned or unplanned. The people's worship in these verses was spontaneous, unplanned. Of course, planned worship services help give structure and coherence to a church service, but God is not limited by church bulletins or orders of service. His Spirit moves over people and genuine, spontaneous worship is the result. But worship in the form of giving must be planned, or often it doesn't happen. If you wait until you have enough to give, you wind up never giving. Both

137

planned and unplanned worship bring pleasure to the giver or the worshiper, and also to God.

True worship also assumes an attitude of submission to God. The Bible tells us, "To obey is better than sacrifice" (1 Samuel 15:22 NKJV). Worship is an act of obedience, like reading and studying God's Word and listening to Him speak to us as we pray. In Hebrew, the idea of sitting at someone's feet meant to learn from a teacher, to listen as a disciple would. When we sit at Jesus' feet, we listen and learn from Him.

Worship should also be sacrificial. The Bible talks about the "sacrifice of praise": "Therefore by Him let us continually offer the sacrifice of praise to God, that is, the fruit of our lips, giving thanks to His name. But do not forget to do good and to share, for with such sacrifices God is well pleased" (Hebrews 13:15-16 NKJV).

True worship is sincere. Whether we sing with our hands in the air or at our sides, whether we clap or remain still, true worship involves the whole person. We're not just going through the motions; instead, we are focusing on God and all He has done for us. The natural response to God's goodness is praise and worship.

Worship can occur anywhere: at home, in church, in the car, on the beach, or at work. Cultivating a worshipful lifestyle means we try to be always aware of God's presence, turning to Him naturally and often as we go about our lives.

While worship styles differ, it is a practice God loves and desires. When we open our hands and our hearts, we receive from Him, but we also give back to Him what belongs to Him—our worship.

What about You? Is your worship spontaneous, submissive, and sacrificial? Is it free from criticism of others who may choose to worship in other ways than you do?

Try a new form of worship today. In your Bible study time, sing a hymn or write a poem to God. Experiment in your own home with various worship postures as you pray: kneeling, standing, lying prostrate before God.

Take a Look Find five reasons in Psalm 33 that God is worthy of our worship.

INQUIRING MINDS

 Thomas said to Him, "Lord, we do not know where You are going, and how can we know the way?" Jesus said to him, "I am the way, the truth, and the life. No one comes to the Father except through Me." John 14:5-6 NKJV

DOUBTING THOMAS is a person who has made his way into our common language, often referred to as the guy whose faith failed him. But Thomas was really just a man with questions, questions he had the courage to ask.

Have you ever been in a classroom or a training situation with a question, but you figure everyone knows the answer but you? You hesitate to raise your hand and ask because you don't want to look foolish?

Thomas subscribed to the adage, "There are no stupid questions." He wanted to know, so he asked. And Jesus answered him simply and straightforwardly with a statement of who He was and why He is sufficient (the way, the truth, the life, and the pathway to God).

After the Resurrection, Thomas wanted proof that Jesus was really Jesus. Instead of lambasting Thomas for his failure to believe, Jesus simply showed him His hands and His side where He had been pierced, letting him see for himself that His wounds were real. Thomas immediately believed and Jesus said it's even better when someone believes without seeing proof.

God is obviously able to handle our doubts. He is not upset by them, and He understands that we have them. Thomas didn't reveal anything Jesus didn't already know when he asked his questions, and neither do we when we bring honest, soul-felt questions to God. He's fully capable of answering.

Every believer at some time experiences doubt; it's part of being human and being in relationship with someone invisible.

Admitting doubt can be the first step to faith and is a key ingredient in having a genuine faith instead of just pretense. Taking doubts to God can be a turning point when a person makes faith his own.

Asking honest questions is different from constantly looking for holes or inconsistencies in the Scriptures and becoming cynical, and it's different from repeatedly asking, "Why me?" The latter indicates that the asker is somehow entitled to different treatment from everyone else, that bad things aren't supposed to happen in his or her life. While the more appropriate question could be "Why not me?" God even understands our feelings of desperation and despair revealed in the "Why me?" query.

God is the God of the intellectual, the God of the scientist, the God of the lawyer. Believers don't have to check their brains at the door before entering church because God is able to undergo the most rigorous scrutiny. What we can ask, He can surely answer.

What about You? Are you honest with God? Do you ask Him your hard questions or are you afraid that you'll make Him mad or show the weakness of your faith?

Thomas showed us that we can take our thorniest questions to God in prayer. He doesn't mind, and like a good teacher, He is only too glad to help us with our questions as we study His Word to find the answers.

Take a Look Read Job chapters 38 and 39 and find at least ten questions asked by God.

CHURCH OR CLUB

 I am the true vine, and My Father is the vinedresser. Every branch in Me that does not bear fruit He takes away; and every branch that bears fruit He prunes, that it may bear more fruit. John 15:1-2 NKJV

TRACEY SHOOK HANDS with the friendly man greeting people as they entered the big church. "Welcome to Grace Church," he said with a smile. Tracey stepped into the large foyer as the greeter reached for the next hand in the line of people coming into the church. Her frayed coat was in its fourth season of hard wear, and she couldn't help noticing how nice everyone looked. It seemed as if each person she saw was dressed in what Tracey thought must be designer clothing, they looked so elegant. *I'm definitely the poorest person here,* she thought. *But that's okay. Jesus loves us all the same.*

Tracey found a seat in the beautiful auditorium with its high ceilings and wooden pews. A family of four sat down next to her, the two toddlers squirming on their parents' laps. The mother smiled at Tracey and continued her discussion with her husband about their upcoming vacation to the Bahamas. The service hadn't started yet, but Tracey fought an almost uncontrollable urge to bolt from the pew and go home. *Everyone here is so successful, and I can barely make ends meet.*

Tracey managed to stay for the entire service and appreciated the choir's music and the pastor's sermon on what it really means to love one's neighbor. After the service, the toddlers' parents scurried out of church, relieved that their struggle to keep two little children quiet was just about over.

Tracey never went back to Grace Church. She just couldn't shake the thought that she was the only person there who wasn't rich.

While Christians don't need to dress shabbily or pretend to be poor, churches need to fight against an appearance of spiritual elitism that goes much deeper than the economic level of its members. Spiritual elitism occurs when a Pharisaical attitude creeps in, an attitude that says, "We're pretty mature in this church. We're not really an outreach church or a teaching church because we're all mature believers who know the Bible."

Spiritual elitism leaves no room for genuine Christianity. Jesus said that productivity is a mark of a believer or a church properly connected to God. In John 15 He explains that the smug vine that isn't producing anything will be cut off, and even the productive vine will be shaped by the pruning knife to make it even more effective.

A church filled with so-called mature believers who aren't producing much and who don't think they need to learn anything new is a nonproductive vine that will be cut away. It is not properly connected to God if its productivity consists of a potluck once a month and a capital campaign to build a new church building. The vine Jesus talks about is real and alive; it's growing and changing, becoming more productive because of the nourishment it receives from God and the sometimes painful care He gives.

Churches need people at every level of Christianity: the curious who are looking for Him and may not even know it, the newborn babes in Christ, those who are a bit further along the path with Him, those who are struggling and doubting, and those who have walked with Him for many years and found Him faithful.

Homogeneity can be boring. If everyone's the same, we miss out on the rich cross-cultural relationships and experiences that we'll surely have in heaven where people of every tribe and nation will dwell together in harmony.

Celebrating differences can be a way to dispel spiritual elitism and breathe some fresh air into a church because, as Tracey

knew, in reality we are all the same in Christ, forgiven sinners
with a long way still to go.

What about You? Give yourself an attitude check. Do you
talk like you're humble and genuine, but deep down you think
you've really arrived as a Christian? Do you know so many
Bible verses that you can come up with one for every occasion
from memory, so you don't really need to read the Bible much
anymore?

   One mark of true maturity is humility, a willingness to learn,
and an understanding that we never really arrive in the Christian life until we get to heaven. Ask God to give you the mind of
Christ so that you can see both things and other people from
His perspective.

Take a Look Read 1 Corinthians 12:12-19 and write down a
benefit of accepting differences among believers.

ASKING AND ANSWERING

 Most assuredly, I say to you, whatever you ask the Father in My name He will give you. Until now you have asked nothing in My name. Ask, and you will receive, that your joy may be full. John 16:23-24 NKJV

STATISTICS TELL US that 95 percent of Americans believe in prayer. Yet so many are just talking to the ceiling because without the Spirit of Christ, without the powerful name of the genuine Jesus, we have no promise of answered prayer. God listens to those who come in the name of His beloved Son, those whose lives are committed to Him.

We don't need to be eloquent, and we don't need to use certain words. In fact, the Bible says that even if all we can do is groan, God's Spirit takes our speechless prayers to the throne of God as powerful petitions (Romans 8:26). He translates our deepest need and relays it to God. Sometimes life hurts so much that all we can do is say, "Jesus, help me." We are too wounded and weak to describe the situation in words.

Think of prayer as a turning circle propelled by God. He has a purpose in His heart to accomplish something here on earth through you. He sends the desire to your heart through His Holy Spirit, and you then pray about that desire, taking it right back to God.

The psalmist tells us, "Delight yourself also in the LORD, and He shall give you the desires of your heart" (Psalm 37:4 NKJV). He plants a desire in our hearts, and then He fulfills the desire.

But how do we know if our desires line up with God's? Is it enough to pray about something, and tell yourself that since you have a peaceful feeling about it, it must be God's will? No, praying is important, but your desires must conform to what God says in the Bible or they are not from Him. A desire for another person's spouse, no matter now much peace you feel about it, is not a desire from God. A plan to gain a large sum of money by cheating in a business deal, even if you can rationalize it a hundred different ways, is not a plan from God.

If what you desire is not specifically addressed in the Bible—whether to go into your own business, for example—prayer should be accompanied by a great deal of research, financial calculation, and advice from wise and experienced people.

Jesus says in John 16:23 that God gives us whatever we ask in His name. But notice that the next sentence says, "Ask, and you will receive, that your joy may be full." In other words, He gives us what He knows will ultimately give us joy, what is best for us, not just what we think we want. As children learn in Sunday school, God gives three different answers to our prayers, *Yes, No,* or *Wait,* depending on what is best for us. He can see the future and we can't, and He does what is best for our long-term good.

Try to find everything the Bible says about the greatest desire of your heart. Once you know it is something God approves of, place it before His throne, asking Him in Jesus' name to fulfill it. He doesn't promise to answer according to our timetable, but He does promise to answer our requests in the very best way.

What about You? What is your prayer life like? Do you approach God reverently, yet boldly, expecting Him to answer? Do you ask without expecting much? Or do you not even bother to ask at all, except in an emergency?

Jesus tells us that the Father will answer our prayers, but we need to ask in order to be answered. Renew your prayer life today by writing out your prayer requests, leaving room to note when and how they are answered.

Take a Look Look up Matthew 17:20-21 and find a key ingredient in powerful prayer.

A GOOD NAME

Pilate went outside again and said to the people, "I am going to bring him out to you now, but understand clearly that I find him not guilty." Then Jesus came out wearing the crown of thorns and the purple robe. And Pilate said, "Here is the man!" When they saw him, the leading priests and Temple guards began shouting, "Crucify! Crucify!" "You crucify him," Pilate said. "I find him not guilty." John 19:4-6

PASTOR SCOTT WAS STUNNED when Cheryl Ames stood up at the church business meeting and complained about his handling of pastoral duties. "My daughter was critically ill, and he didn't call for over two weeks. His neglect really hurt." Scott's congregation consisted of more than two thousand people, and he hadn't even known about Cheryl's daughter's illness.

Next, Bob stood to say that he didn't think Scott had the pastoral quality of mercy because Scott had insisted that Bob's pregnant daughter and her boyfriend get premarital counseling before their wedding. According to Bob, this counseling had delayed their marriage by four weeks during which time their predicament became even more visible.

As Scott listened to the accusations, he felt as though his reputation was being shattered, his four years of hard work and loving sacrifice to this church wiped out in one business meeting. Wouldn't anyone stand up and tell the truth about him?

Reputation. A good name. In Proverbs we read, "A good name is to be chosen rather than great riches, loving favor rather than silver and gold" (Proverbs 22:1 NKJV). Everyone wants a good reputation. But think of the ultimate Good Person, Jesus Christ. He certainly should have had the best reputation of anyone ever, because He had never sinned. And yet He was maligned.

In John 19:4-6, Pilate found no guilt in Jesus, but His own people—the Jewish leaders—attacked Him anyway.

The reputation of Jesus has taken many twists and turns over the course of history. Napoleon said, "I know men and Jesus was no mere man." Strauss, the German rationalist, called Jesus "the highest model of religion." John Stewart Mills said, "Jesus was the guide of humanity." The French atheist Renan said Jesus was "the greatest among the sons of men." Theodore Parker said, "Jesus was a youth, with God in His heart." H. G. Wells placed Jesus Christ at the top of the list of the ten greatest human beings in history.

Jesus' true reputation as Son of God and Savior of the world has lasted over the millennia. But the religious leaders of His day still said, "Crucify Him."

First Peter 2:19-20 says, "For God is pleased with you when, for the sake of your conscience, you patiently endure unfair treatment. Of course, you get no credit for being patient if you are beaten for doing wrong. But if you suffer for doing right and are patient beneath the blows, God is pleased with you." Clearly, when we do wrong, we will suffer for it. We deserve a bad reputation if we continually hurt others or are dishonest or deceitful.

But sometimes reputations are damaged or even destroyed based on no wrongdoing, and these verses urge us to endure them patiently, as Jesus did in John 19.

What about You? What about your reputation? Do you live in such a way to have a good reputation, trying to be at peace with all and confessing and making right the wrongs you do? If so, has your reputation ever been tarnished unjustly? What did you do about it?

Jesus patiently endured accusation, knowing that God the Father knew His true reputation and His opinion was all that really mattered. Take your reputation to Him today, and ask Him to help you patiently endure unfair criticism.

SECTION 3: KING OF MY WORLD

Take a Look "You hide them in the shelter of your presence, safe from those who conspire against them. You shelter them in your presence, far from accusing tongues" (Psalm 31:20).

Look up James 1:26 and James 3:8-10. Write down two truths about the importance of what we say.

SECTION 4

Lover of My Soul

REAL LIFE WITH THE REAL GOD

 In the beginning the Word already existed. He was with God, and he was God. He was in the beginning with God. He created everything there is. Nothing exists that he didn't make.
John 1:1-3

WHEN PETER'S GRANDFATHER died, the family found an old, beat-up violin in his attic. No one even knew the grandfather had ever played the violin or any other instrument. Peter was shocked when he turned the violin over and found the Latin inscription, *Antonius Stradivarius Cremonensis Faciebat Anno 1727,* which gives the maker (Antonio Stradivari), the place (Cremonia, Italy), and the year of manufacture.

Peter excitedly began to research Stradivarius violins, hoping he had discovered a treasure. He learned that of the 1,100 instruments Stradivari made 250 years ago, 512 violins are known to have survived. Could he have the 513th in his hand? Imagine his disappointment when, based on its analysis of the details, the wood, and the craftsmanship of the instrument, the appraisal by the American Federation of Violin and Bow Makers labeled his grandfather's violin a mere copy. It looked genuine, but it was a fake.

The apostle John begins his story of Jesus' life by telling us something so specific, so exact, about how God has revealed Himself to us that there can be no doubt as to Jesus' authenticity. God came to earth to make Himself known to mankind in the person of Jesus of Nazareth. That fact becomes the central reason why we believe in Jesus—because Jesus is God. He has always existed, before everything we know of today. He is the real God.

The most profound statement anyone can make is to say that a person is God. And yet John said it, without apology or

155

hesitancy, about Jesus. He called Jesus "the Word," which in John's day meant a controlling idea or concept. A word is what we use to express an idea, to verbalize something we are thinking. A word is an audible expression of an invisible meaning. And in that same sense, Jesus of Nazareth was the living Word of God. He came to earth to reveal the will, words, and works of God to mankind.

But He wasn't just a representative of God, as some have claimed. He was God. When John says, "He was with God," he means that Jesus was face-to-face with God and had to leave that position and the glory of heaven to come to earth and be God among us.

If we went into any shopping mall in America and asked the question, "Yes or no: Do you believe in Jesus?" I can assure you we would get a majority of positive responses. Based on the evidence, however, it seems that we're not all believing in the same Jesus. Unless our definition of Jesus includes the fact that He is God, we are not talking about the Jesus Christ of Scripture.

What does it mean in your life that Jesus is the genuine God?

The apostle John actually walked on earth with Jesus. He traveled with Him, ate with Him, and talked intimately with Him. John refers to himself as "the disciple whom Jesus loved" (John 21:7). John wasn't bragging about his favored position with Jesus; he was expressing his amazement that Jesus loved him.

And we can all say what John said. We are also disciples whom Jesus loves. We, too, can travel with Him, eat with Him, and talk with Him intimately, because He is as close as our breath. He knows our every thought, and not a thing we do or experience escapes His notice.

Because Jesus is God, your life can be dramatically different. You have access to the power of God every day because you know and are loved by His Son. But access is not the same as experience. You must do something to access His power. He is there, waiting to come into your life. "Behold, I stand at the door and knock. If anyone hears My voice and opens the door, I will come in to him and dine with him, and he with Me" (Revelation 3:20 NKJV). Are you ready to invite Jesus into your life?

What about You? God came to earth and has given you every reason to believe. Do you believe, really believe? Is your faith an intellectual matter consisting of facts and Bible verses? Or, like John, have you rested your head on Jesus' shoulder, accepted the vast love He has for you, and become a disciple whom He loves? Open the door today; He's waiting with open arms.

Take a Look To learn more about Jesus and His power, read Hebrews 1. Find at least three statements about the everlasting nature of God.

SPEAKING MY LANGUAGE

 So the Word became human and lived here on earth among us. He was full of unfailing love and faithfulness. And we have seen his glory, the glory of the only Son of the Father.
John 1:14

WHEN MY DAUGHTER, Kelly, was in college, she flew to Mexico to participate in Spanish language studies because her goal was to become a bilingual schoolteacher. The best and fastest way to really learn the language—complete with all the cultural nuances unavailable in textbooks—was to immerse herself in a Hispanic environment for an extended period.

Kelly had to board a plane, travel many miles, and get face-to-face with Spanish-speaking people. She couldn't learn the language from afar because she didn't want her "foreignness" to be a problem for the Hispanic students she would teach. She wanted to be able to communicate fluently and effectively, so she left her American culture and traveled to a Hispanic culture to live and learn about life there.

In a miraculous way, God immersed Himself in our culture. In order to communicate His love to a hurting human race, He became a genuine human being. He could have communicated with us from afar, but He chose to do it up close, leaving His own heavenly "culture" and immersing Himself in ours as one of us. That's who Jesus Christ is—the genuine God who came to earth and pitched His tent right in the middle of us. He spoke our language.

Bible scholar William Barclay calls this verse "the most profound thought and theme of Scripture." God showed us His glory in the form of His Son who laid aside the prerogatives and privileges of deity and limited Himself to a human body. He descended from heaven and condescended to mankind.

Instead of communicating with people through messengers as God did in the Old Testament, Jesus came to be grace and truth in person (Hebrews 1:1-2). Born in a stable—a barn, not in a magnificent hospital with great prenatal care and the latest technology—He came to a poor family. And contrary to the pretty pictures of the nativity scene, the barn wasn't clean or sweet-smelling. Since He did not live in luxury, He can relate to everyone, of every economic level, from every social stratum, and in every circumstance. He was still God, but He took on the form of a human. He laid aside His dignity, but not His deity.

When I became a father for the first time, I didn't cease to be a husband, and I didn't cease to be a man. But I took on fatherhood in addition to those other roles. When God became man, He did not become less than God, but He took on human flesh, in addition to being God. The invisible God became visible. He grew from baby to child to teenager to adult, experiencing the same feelings and temptations we experience.

His human experience was thoroughly real. He knows our pain and our joy because He speaks our language.

What about You? Do you ever feel misunderstood? Like you want someone who really understands what you're going through? Jesus knows where you are, and even better, He understands how you feel in that spot. He speaks your language, the language of God's love.

Take a Look Read the Beatitudes in Matthew 5:1-12 for some of Jesus' most eloquent words. Meditate on the principles in these verses to find some of God's most wonderful promises.

NO LONGER ALONE

 For the law was given through Moses; God's unfailing love and faithfulness came through Jesus Christ. John 1:17

MARIA WAS one of the millions of street orphans roaming the streets of Brazil in packs. She didn't know her age; she could hardly remember her mother. Her older brother had disappeared from the village shortly after her mother died and her younger sister had died of a terrible disease that seemed to just shrivel up her life. Maria had little to hope for, only that she might find food today and live until tomorrow.

When the missionary woman gave her food and motioned to her to come sleep in a hut on the mission compound, Maria willingly followed, not knowing whom she followed. The missionary was showing God's love to the little girl, although the child didn't know it at the time.

Most of us are not orphans, wandering alone and searching for food. But in a way we are: Without God we have no heavenly Father, we sometimes feel alone, and we futilely search for what will fill our cavernous hunger. Yet all we need—God's unfailing love and faithfulness—was provided in the form of Jesus. Once we understand this, we no longer need to wander around, frightened and alone.

What does this mean for you today, knowing that God's unfailing love and faithfulness came to us through Jesus Christ?

First, it means that God loves you very much. By sending His Son to earth, He proved that His love was genuine (John 3:16). Never again do you need to wonder how God feels about you. You need only to look at Jesus and be assured of God's love.

Second, it means that God understands what you go through in life because Jesus experienced it all. He was tempted by the devil (Matthew 4:1-11) just as we are tempted and He suffered (Hebrews 5:8) just as we suffer. On your worst days, in your most trying times, you can be assured that Jesus has been there before you and He knows what it's like to cry out in emotional or physical pain.

Third, it means that Jesus represents you before the Father, acting as your go-between with God (1 Timothy 2:5-6) and as your advocate. He can also empower you to please God by living a life of obedience.

The apostle Paul said that Jesus' birth as a baby was a great mystery of our faith (1 Timothy 3:16). It's hard for us to understand why He would want to immerse Himself in our lives, our world, and our struggles. But because He did, we are no longer alone. He paved the way for us to know God.

What about You? Do you ever feel lost, alone, and empty, unsure which way to turn? At times like these, remember that Jesus is with you every minute, so you're never alone or without any resources. Jesus will hear even your feeblest call for help and rush to your side to help you. God's unfailing love and faithfulness are there for you in Jesus, even when you feel like an aimless wanderer.

Take a Look In Isaiah 30:21 we are promised that God will continue to teach and guide us: "You will hear a voice say, 'This is the way; turn around and walk here.'" Sometimes He speaks to us in a still, small voice or a gentle whisper (1 Kings 19:12). List areas of concern where you most need guidance from God in your life.

LIVING WATER

A woman of Samaria came to draw water. Jesus said to her, "Give Me a drink." For His disciples had gone away into the city to buy food. Then the woman of Samaria said to Him, "How is it that You, being a Jew, ask a drink from me, a Samaritan woman?" For Jews have no dealings with Samaritans. Jesus answered and said to her, "If you knew the gift of God, and who it is who says to you, 'Give Me a drink,' you would have asked Him, and He would have given you living water." John 4:7-10 NKJV

SHE WAS used to rejection. She was accustomed to being ignored. The woman at the well was not only a despised, mixed-race Samaritan, she was also living with a man to whom she was not married, after having had five husbands. She came to the well in the heat of the day to avoid the other women who socialized there evenings and who would surely shun her. She expected no respectable Jewish man to speak to her because Jewish men never spoke to women in public, especially not a Samaritan woman of her reputation. Imagine her surprise when Jesus asked her for a drink.

But her background didn't matter to Him—He entered her world, and He talked about things she would understand. He overcame the racial, cultural, and religious barriers that existed between Him, a Jew, and her, a Samaritan. He asked for a drink and spoke to her with dignity and respect. His speech was plain talk, not religious jargon, and she responded.

She had not heard of this stranger nor seen His miracles. At first she was probably suspicious. But when He mentioned living water, she was interested. Perhaps her interest was because she had been to the wells of this world many times, attempting to quench her thirst with the love of a man. By now she had discovered, in her disillusionment, that those wells were dry. She

163

had probably believed that each husband was Mr. Right and that each marriage would last forever. But her dreams had been crushed and nothing had worked out. She had a hole in her heart, just as all human beings do, that can only be filled by the living God.

Cleverly-disguised dry wells dot our landscape today. One of them is career. Chris worked more than sixty hours a week and had little energy left for his family when he got home at night. His wife, Tracey, wished Chris would spend more time with her and the children, but by concentrating her efforts on meeting the needs of eight-year-old Amy and six-year-old Josh, she found herself plenty busy, even without Chris at home.

A stay-at-home mom, Tracey drove the children to and from school so they wouldn't have to be out in bad weather. She drove them to music and sports lessons and worked with them on their homework every day. She dropped them off at their friends' houses and did errands while they played before she picked them up to go home. She didn't have time to see her friends anymore or to volunteer at church like she used to do because she wanted to be there for her children whenever they needed her.

Chris was dipping into the dry well of career while Tracey based her life on her children. Both began to feel tired and depleted because they were looking for fulfillment in the wrong places. Work and relationships are important and necessary, but they will come up dry if we try to find life's meaning in them. We must quench our thirst only in Jesus, the Living Water that never runs dry, not in our jobs or other people, no matter how highly we value them.

What about You? What empty wells have you been drawing from in an effort to slake your thirst? The well of personal achievement? Pleasure? Money? Have you thought, *If I can just get that promotion, or get married, or get married to someone else, or buy a new house—then I'll be happy?*

Come to the splashing, deep, delicious well of Jesus Christ and dip into the living water that will end your futile searching at those dry and dusty empty wells.

Take a Look Water has another symbolic purpose in the Bible. In Psalm 51:2 David asks God to wash him clean from guilt and purify him from sin. Read 1 Corinthians 6:11 to see what else the Living Water has done for you.

TIME OUT

Therefore when Jesus perceived that they were about to come and take Him by force to make Him king, He departed again to the mountain by Himself alone. John 6:15 NKJV

AMY GOT UP TO SEE her husband off to work and then headed to the kitchen to start making the children's lunches for school. But the electric garage door awakened the baby when Kevin left, and Amy climbed the stairs to get little Lisa who was crying.

By the time Lisa had finished her bottle, it was time to call Jeffrey and Michelle for breakfast. As first- and third-graders, both children dressed themselves and brushed their teeth and hair, sort of. But on this particular morning Michelle knocked over her cereal bowl, and the milk dripped through the slim gap in the table where the boards came together and soaked the little girl's lavender slacks, prompting her to cry.

By the time Amy took a quick shower and ushered the older children out to the school bus, she knew she would be late for the women's Bible study she taught at church. This was especially frustrating since she would have to leave that meeting early in order to get Lisa to her grandmother's and make it to her part-time job on time. She knew she shouldn't feel so frazzled when she arrived to teach the Bible, and she regretted skipping her prayer and Bible reading time that morning.

The Bible tells us that Jesus went off by Himself to pray often, no matter who was demanding His attention. While Amy couldn't have just ignored her children and disappeared into a closet, she understood the importance of carving out some time in her day for quietness before God.

In John 6 we see that Jesus went up the mountain overlooking the Sea of Galilee, from where He could see everything the disciples did down below. He talked with God the Father and watched over His disciples at the same time. They couldn't see Him, but He saw them.

We can be sure that Jesus is praying for us today. According to Hebrews 7:25 (NKJV), "He always lives to make intercession for them." He sits at the right hand of the Father, and from that place of authority, from that heavenly vantage point, Jesus prays for us. Like the disciples in John 6, we can't see Him, but He sees us and knows who we are and what we need.

Sometimes it seems as if all we can manage in a crisis is a prayer-on-the-run, "Help me, God." But Jesus prayed with focused concentration during stressful or even dangerous times, like in the Garden of Gethsemane when He was about to be betrayed. "He began to be filled with anguish and deep distress. He told them, 'My soul is crushed with grief to the point of death. Stay here and watch with me.' He went on a little farther and fell face down on the ground, praying, 'My Father! If it is possible, let this cup of suffering be taken away from me. Yet I want your will, not mine'" (Matthew 26:37-39).

When the weight of life makes us feel as though we don't have time or strength to pray, we must remember what Jesus did. He prayed often and much, no matter what was going on around Him. He fully understood His genuine need for private time with God the Father.

What about You? Do you get away with God frequently, just the two of you, for close personal time together? A hundred other things vie for our time, and they fought for Jesus' time as well. But He knew the importance of getting alone with His Father, no matter how many people were clamoring for His attention.

Take a Look "Don't worry about anything; instead, pray about everything. Tell God what you need, and thank him for all he has done. If you do this, you will experience God's peace, which is far more wonderful than the human mind can understand. His peace will guard your hearts and minds as you live in Christ Jesus" (Philippians 4:6-7).

List three things you don't pray about because you think they're too insignificant to bother God with. Then put them under the "everything" category we're told here to pray about.

COME TO THE TABLE

 Jesus replied, "I am the bread of life. No one who comes to me will ever be hungry again. Those who believe in me will never thirst." John 6:35

FARIDA WAS RESTLESS. She had been born and raised in a devout Muslim family in Indonesia. After university, she came to the United States and eventually married a Jewish man. Her sister became a Buddhist, and her grandchildren attended a Christian preschool.

"I'm so confused. I pick and choose from all religions, taking what seems true and letting the rest go. But I feel hungry for something more, something solid I can believe in," she said.

In John 6:35 Jesus offered to satisfy Farida's hunger, to lead her to the truth if she did her part to find it. Farida's Bible reading and Quran reading method is haphazard. She lets the book fall open, closes her eyes, and puts her finger on a verse, believing that particular verse will be the answer to her problem for the day.

But Jesus tells us that He is the Bread, not one of the breads, or part of a spiritual smorgasbord we can select from. Farida needs to ask God to show her the truth and then read the Bible, guided by a Bible study or a church.

God satisfies our deepest hunger and gives us the opportunity to find out who He is and place our faith in Him. But we must do our part in this search-and-find operation. We must look for Him where He can be found. When the children of Israel wandered the desert, they cried out to God for help. They needed food, and He miraculously supplied manna that they found on the ground every morning. In the Old Testament manna is a picture of Jesus, the Bread of heaven who came from God. The round shape of the manna symbolizes the eternality

171

of God. The white color represents Jesus' purity. It was to be gathered every day and eaten, providing sustenance on a daily basis, as we need Jesus every day.

But the Israelites had a choice. They could either walk over the manna or they could pick it up and eat it. We have the same choice today: we can allow God to help us, or not. The Bread of heaven is here and available to us, and we can either take Him into our lives or ignore Him.

Physical bread, or food, sustains us, strengthens us, and enables to live, just as Jesus sustains us spiritually. Without the reality of Jesus in our lives, we are weak, powerless, and lifeless, starved for the only One who can truly satisfy.

What about You? Have you picked up and used the resources God has provided for you? Or do they lie fallow, going to waste due to inattention and lack of care? Have you failed to recognize what He has provided because it's not exactly what you had asked for?

Jesus Christ is heaven's Bread for your hunger, God's provision for all your needs. The choice is yours. Will you allow Him to fill you, sustain you, and energize you? Or will you keep on looking elsewhere for what you crave?

Take a Look Ephesians 3:19 says that you will be filled with the fullness of life and power that comes from God when you experience the love of Christ. Read and meditate on that verse as you thank God for His abundant provision.

TO PRAY OR PREY

 Then Jesus said to them again, "Most assuredly, I say to you, I am the door of the sheep. All who ever came before Me are thieves and robbers, but the sheep did not hear them. I am the door. If anyone enters by Me, he will be saved, and will go in and out and find pasture." John 10:7-9 NKJV

"IF YOU SEND ME fifty dollars with your prayer request, I'll pray for you every day for the next year," the slick televangelist said. Since before the days of Jesus, some religious leaders have misused their positions of authority and trust to take advantage of those in their care. For centuries, certain members of the clergy have cajoled and intimidated people into giving them money, money some could hardly afford to give, allowing the religious leaders to live in luxury while their parishioners struggled to put food on their family's table.

These preying pastors are well known by God. Paul wrote about them in his letter to Titus, "For there are many who rebel against right teaching; they engage in useless talk and deceive people. . . . They must be silenced. By their wrong teaching, they have already turned whole families away from the truth. Such teachers only want your money" (Titus 1:10-11).

The religious leaders in Jesus' day also took money from their followers. But again and again Jesus pointed out their hypocrisy—and yes, their sin—bluntly and clearly. The religious leaders were offended time after time by what He said because what He said was true.

Whether a thief comes in the form of a false or dishonest religious leader, or a temptation to crime, alcoholism, or drug abuse, all thieves come to steal, kill, and destroy (John 10:10). And behind each thief is Satan, offering what seems to be a way of escape from problems; but in reality it's an escape into something much, much worse. While Jesus provides tender care for His sheep, He condemns those religious leaders who would harm their followers, whether they are churchgoers, ministry followers, or impressionable children.

"But whoever causes one of these little ones who believe in Me to stumble, it would be better for him if a millstone were hung around his neck, and he were thrown into the sea" (Mark 9:42 NKJV). God takes misuse of authority seriously, and those who take advantage of people in their care will answer for it.

"These false teachers are like unthinking animals, creatures of instinct, who are born to be caught and killed. They laugh at the terrifying powers they know so little about, and they will be destroyed along with them" (2 Peter 2:12).

What about You? What kind of care are you giving those for whom you are responsible? It could be your children, your employees, or your students. Are you serving as a door to your sheep, leading them with love into green pastures, or are you more like a thief who takes advantage?

Take a good, hard look at your shepherding skills and ask God to make you more like the Good Shepherd who protects, provides, and tenderly cares for His sheep.

Take a Look Read Psalm 34:11-22. Find at least four things a good teacher teaches his followers to do.

PORTRAIT OF A GOOD SHEPHERD

 I am the good shepherd; and I know My sheep, and am known by My own. As the Father knows Me, even so I know the Father; and I lay down My life for the sheep.
John 10:14-15 NKJV

KELLY HAD been a mother for only eighteen months when it happened. Her daughter, Lacey, was toddling near her in the large department store as Kelly looked through a circular rack of children's clothes. Kelly had two one-piece terrycloth garments in her arms when she spoke to Lacey, as she did frequently. But this time there was no answer and no toddler nearby.

Kelly said, "Lacey—where are you, honey?"

No response from the usually chattering child. Kelly's heart constricted as she fought down panic. *She's right nearby, she just can't hear me,* she thought. Kelly walked quickly around the racks of clothes, repeating Lacey's name louder and louder, fear inching up her throat.

Kelly was just about to call for help and ask the store security to lock all exits to the store when movement in one of the clothing racks caught her eye. A tiny hand reached out to part the clothes and a smiling Lacey said, "Peek-boo, Mama," her baby version of the game the two played together. Relief flooded Kelly as she scooped up the child with a prayer of thanks and an admonishment to always answer when Mama calls her name.

Just as a parent would not stop until she had exhausted every possible way to search for her lost child, Jesus, the Good Shepherd, cares for every one of His sheep. In Luke 15:4-5, He said, "If you had one hundred sheep, and one of them strayed away and was lost in the wilderness, wouldn't you leave the ninety-nine others to go and search for the lost one until you found it? And then you would joyfully carry it home on your shoulders."

The Good Shepherd leads His sheep tenderly, lovingly, and personally. In John 10:14-15 Jesus referred to a sheepfold, a crude enclosure made of rocks and sticks. The door was not an actual door or a gate, but merely an opening through which the sheep could go in and out. At night the shepherd would lie across the opening, protecting his sheep from intruding predators and from their own tendency to wander away in the night. When He said, "I lay down My life for the sheep," He created a picture of sacrifice on behalf of the flock, as He freely and voluntarily gave His life as a sacrifice for us, His sheep. Jesus contrasts the real shepherd with the hired hand (verses 12-13) who is just in it for the money and does not care about the sheep. The hired man flees when danger approaches while the genuine shepherd stays when the going gets tough.

The job of a shepherd is a humble one, but one that seems to have special significance for God. Some of the greatest men in history have been shepherds. Moses, the lawgiver, was a shepherd. David, the singer and king, was a shepherd. The angel appeared to the shepherds on the night of Christ's birth. Perhaps God's choice of shepherds underscores His desire for the humility, tenderness, and loving care that shepherds give their sheep.

What about You? Jesus said His sheep know Him and recognize His voice. Do you recognize His voice amid the cacophony of life? Do you take time to listen for Him as He tenderly calls your name?

Stop now and picture Jesus Christ, the Good Shepherd, calling for you, leading you, protecting you. Relax into His arms, knowing that even if you feel lost, He will search you out and bring you back to Himself. Trust Him to lead you safely on the journey He has planned for you.

Take a Look Find at least five benefits of being a sheep in the fold of the Good Shepherd that can be found in Psalm 23.

A TIME FOR TEARS

 Therefore, when Jesus saw her weeping, and the Jews who came with her weeping, He groaned in the spirit and was troubled. And He said, "Where have you laid him?" They said to Him, "Lord, come and see." Jesus wept.
John 11:33-35 NKJV

WHAT MAKES YOU CRY?

I cried with joy when my bride came down the aisle on our wedding day. Then the first time I held each of my children, I cried because I was overcome with the joy of being a father. I cried with sorrow when my father died and again when my mother died. Significant times of life are often marked by tears of joy or tears of sorrow. Tears are a part of the human experience.

Being fully God and yet fully man, Jesus experienced all the feelings we do. He understands our joys and sorrows because He has been there Himself and He is there with us in the midst of our hard times.

In the early years of the church, the Gnostics claimed that Jesus was not human. They believed that since everything physical was evil, God could not take on human flesh and become contaminated with sin. This heresy said Jesus was a sort of spirit phantom, not God in the flesh.

But He was fully human, though fully God. He breathed life into us, and yet He grew tired and He slept. He created the world, and yet He felt physical pain as well as hunger and thirst. He commanded the wind and the waves and they obeyed Him, and yet He laughed and He cried as we do.

In John 11:35 Jesus knew He was going to restore Lazarus to life, but He was overwhelmed with the emotion of the moment and the sadness of all those with Him who were grieving. He was doubtless saddened by this reminder of the ultimate result of sin in the world: death.

Sometimes well-intentioned people say Christians shouldn't cry, even at a funeral. Trying to help, they pat a grieving person on the back and say, "Don't cry. It's going to be okay." Or they might even quote a Bible verse to the person, such as, "All things work together for good to those who love God, to those who are called according to His purpose" (Romans 8:28 NKJV), or "In everything give thanks; for this is the will of God in Christ Jesus for you" (1 Thessalonians 5:18 NKJV). But such a cavalier use of God's Word does little to comfort and may even hurt a wounded person.

During times of great emotion, Jesus gave His presence, His compassion, and His tears. He acknowledged the grief of Lazarus's loved ones by His own emotional response.

As Jesus called Lazarus back from the dead, He knew what it was like to be in the perfection of heaven, as Lazarus was right then, and then to come to earth with all its depravity, sin, and pain. Jesus had been in heaven, worshiped by the saints and angels, and then He came to the comparative squalor of earth. He understood what it would be like for Lazarus to have to leave that glorious place and return here. No matter how much we'd like to bring our deceased loved ones back to this life, we know they're in a far better place in heaven with God. Perhaps part of the reason Jesus cried was that He knew what Lazarus would have to leave when he came back to life.

Even though Jesus knew the end of the story—He knew that Lazarus would live again and that one day "God will wipe away every tear from their eyes; there shall be no more death, nor sorrow, nor crying" (Revelation 21:4 NKJV)—His tears revealed His humanity. They represented His sympathy, they recognized the tragedy of sin, and they reflected the glory of heaven.

And for us reading about the death and restored life of Lazarus, Jesus' tears remind us once again that His love and compassion are real.

What about You? Have you given yourself, your friends, your loved ones, and your children permission to cry when they're sad? Are you willing to express your emotions in a healthy and respectful way?

Jesus wasn't ashamed to cry, and He made us with that ability as well—the ability to feel joy and sadness and a host of other emotions. Ask Him to help you feel those marvelous feelings He put inside of you, to help you to express them appropriately, and to share in the feelings of others as well.

Take a Look Read Psalm 30:1-12. What did David learn about weeping and sorrow as described in this psalm?

THE BELIEVER'S BADGE

 A new commandment I give to you, that you love one another; as I have loved you, that you also love one another. By this all will know that you are My disciples, if you have love for one another. John 13:34-35 NKJV

RON HAD WORN his WWJD bracelet for so long that its edges were frayed. He hardly noticed the reminder to ask himself *What Would Jesus Do?* anymore because the bracelet had become just another part of his daily attire, like his shoes and socks.

If someone asked him about the bracelet, he gave a good answer about Jesus and how he wanted to be like Him. But when no one was asking, Ron's thoughts were usually far from this symbol of his faith.

The bracelet occupied its usual spot on his right wrist when a driver from another lane cut Ron off on his way home from work. Ron leaned on his horn and yelled, "What do you think you're doing?" as if the driver could hear his words in his air-conditioned car with the windows up.

The other driver made an obscene hand signal, and Ron felt his face grow hot with anger. Since he was a Christian, he would never consider returning the gesture, but he accelerated until he was right on the bumper of the offending car, gripping the steering wheel and glaring. He stayed plastered to the car's bumper, honking intermittently and shaking his fist until the driver exited the freeway a mile later.

Ron wore his WWJD bracelet as a badge of his Christianity, but it didn't do much to advertise his faith on the freeway that day. Jesus said the true mark of a Christian is behavior that demonstrates love.

In John 13 the occasion was the last time the disciples would share a meal with Jesus before His death, the Last Supper. The disciples knew that Jesus' time of departure was drawing near, and they might have been hoping that this was the time Jesus would take charge and establish His kingdom.

Instead, He stooped to wash their feet and explain again what He wanted them to do. He wanted them to be known by their love, not by the emblems of authority worn by the Romans, not by the pious words of the Pharisees, but by humility and love. He adopted the posture of a slave when He washed their feet. He created a picture of love: pouring out one's life for others in selfless, sacrificial, random acts of kindness, doing whatever was necessary to meet the needs of people—not because they deserved it, but because they needed it.

Love is not a feeling; it is action and attitude. One wise college literature professor said, "Love is desiring and working toward the highest spiritual good of the beloved." In other words, love is wanting another to grow into the person God made him or her to be.

When we think about *What Would Jesus Do?* the answer is quite simple. He would do whatever showed love and compassion. He would give true and sacrificial love that never ends.

What about You? Is your life marked by love? Would those who live and work with you say that a hallmark of your life is love? What about other drivers who see you in action on the road?

If you wear a visible symbol of Christianity, make sure your behavior matches up, because if it doesn't, the symbol can repel rather than attract others to Jesus.

Take a Look Read "the love chapter," 1 Corinthians 13 and write down at least ten characteristics of genuine love.

EVIL OVERTURNED

 Then the detachment of troops and the captain and the officers of the Jews arrested Jesus and bound Him. And they led Him away to Annas first, for he was the father-in-law of Caiaphas who was high priest that year. Now it was Caiaphas who advised the Jews that it was expedient that one man should die for the people. John 18:12-14 NKJV

CERTAINLY THE HORRORS of Hitler and his National Socialist Party are among the great evils of all time. Many have wondered why God permitted such atrocity, and we won't fully know the answer until we arrive in eternity and can ask Him. But we do know that since sin entered the world in the Garden of Eden, it has wreaked havoc, brought pain, and caused untold suffering throughout history.

And yet, as always, God brought good from evil. One Christian who defied the Nazis and paid for it with his life was Dietrich Bonhoeffer, a scholar who was a leader in the Confessing Church and an advocate on behalf of the Jews.

Pastor Martin Niemöller, joined Bonhoeffer in forming the Pastors Emergency League later known as the Confessing Church. He said, "First they came for the Jews, and I didn't speak out—because I was not a Jew. Then they came for the Communists, and I did not speak out—because I was not a Communist. Then they came for the trade unionists, and I did not speak out—because I was not a trade unionist. Then they came for me and there was no one left to speak for me!"

The League tried to stop the Nazi manipulation of the churches, and they believed that the exclusion of Jews from the church community was a violation of Christian teaching. Members of the Confessing Church helped approximately two thousand Jews escape to freedom; they also helped political dissidents and Christians persecuted by the Nazis. Bonhoeffer even worked with members of the military resistance who attempted to assassinate Hitler in his Wolf's Lair headquarters. He was hanged in the concentration camp at Flossenbürg on April 9, 1945.

When man did his worst, God did His best. During the horrors of Hitler's day, God found great people of real courage and conviction to stand against the tide of evil.

Jesus' death on the cross as payment for the sins of mankind was God's very best, wrought from man's worst evil: Jesus' betrayal, arrest, false charges at His trial, corrupt court, and crucifixion. His entire human life had been lived for this moment.

Bringing the best from man's worst is one of God's specialties, and He's just as good at it today as He was at the time of the Cross and at the time of the Nazis.

What about You? Is there an event in your life that was unfathomably bad, something that raised questions with no answers, where evil seemed to knock good on its head?

Perhaps you haven't seen one iota of good come from the tragedy and can't even imagine anything good coming from it. Will you trust God even if you have no idea what possible good He will someday bring out of your pain? Ask Him to give you the faith to take His promises to heart and the patience to wait for as long as it takes for Him to keep them.

Take a Look Read Isaiah 5:20-24 to find out what will eventually happen to evildoers.

ART OR AGONY

It was now about noon of the day of preparation for the Passover. And Pilate said to the people, "Here is your king!" "Away with him," they yelled. "Away with him—crucify him!" "What? Crucify your king?" Pilate asked. "We have no king but Caesar," the leading priests shouted back. Then Pilate gave Jesus to them to be crucified. So they took Jesus and led him away. Carrying the cross by himself, Jesus went to the place called Skull Hill (in Hebrew, Golgotha). John 19:14-17

THE CROSS: A SYMBOL of shame and pain and victory. A symbol worn as jewelry and carved as art, the cross has become familiar to believers and nonbelievers alike. But even profound words or objects can lose some of their meaning when they become everyday, commonplace, or ordinary. Words we hear often can start to sound like the overused and under-meant phrase, "How are you?"

But when actor Bruce Marchiano played the role of Jesus Christ in *The Gospel According to Matthew,* he gained a firsthand perspective on why the cross must never become commonplace in the Christian experience. He learned in a small way what it must have been like for Jesus to go to the cross on our behalf.

In an interview about the movie, Marchiano said, "During an eighteen-hour day of filming, I hung on the cross for about eight hours. I expected to get hurt physically, but what I didn't expect was the emotional and spiritual devastation of feeling absolutely alone. No one would come near me. I had spit dripping down my face, and the crowd was laughing. I didn't hear the director call 'action' just before someone grabbed my left hand, put a nail in the center of my palm, and raised the hammer. My universe split at that moment, a moment of horror. Then, to get a sense of reality, they kicked the platform out from under me. It all seemed too real in that instant.

"Then the Lord whispered to me, 'Kid, do you think this is tough for you? This is not even a tiny fraction of what I went through two thousand years ago. But I did it for you. I did it for you.'

"When one of the Roman soldiers looked up at me and said with a laugh, 'If you're the Son of God, come down off the cross,' it hit me with unexpected force: Jesus could have come down any time He decided He had had enough torture. In Matthew 26:53 (NKJV) He said, 'Or do you think that I cannot now pray to My Father, and He will provide Me with more than twelve legions of angels?'

"He could have looked down the tunnel of time and said, 'That guy Bruce is a rebel and he isn't worth it.' I asked myself why, why would the Son of the Living God with all the power in the universe behind Him do a thing like that? Why would He be willing to be separated from God the Father for the first and only time in all eternity?

"And the little phrase that has become almost trite came to me, 'Because I love you. You're worth it.'"

Bruce Marchiano learned a valuable lesson about the price that was paid for his sins when Jesus went to the cross. What does Jesus ask in return? How can we show our astounded gratitude for what He has done?

He said, "If anyone desires to come after Me, let him deny himself, and take up his cross, and follow Me" (Matthew 16:24 NKJV). What is the cross we're to carry? It's not our problems, or a difficult person, or a bad habit. Taking up our cross means being willing to put aside our own personal ambitions, desires, and selfish whims in favor of obeying God, publicly identifying with Him, and living the life of love He showed us.

It is impossible for us to put ourselves in Jesus' place on the cross. He endured it in reality; we can only imagine what it must have been like for Him. But we can all identify with voluntarily doing something hard. If we're honest, we know that if it became too hard, we would probably change our minds and end our suffering.

But not Jesus. He really could have come down, but He didn't. Because He loves you with a true love beyond our understanding. And because you're worth it.

What about You? Are you committed to following Christ even when it's hard to do? Has He called you to do something you are avoiding because it's just too difficult?

He doesn't ask us to do something without supplying the strength to obey. Are you willing to say yes to the task you've been putting off, the difficult job that could really cost you? Tell God you're willing and ask Him to give you the strength and determination to move forward and stay the course even when the going gets rough.

Take a Look In Galatians 2:19-20 Paul describes how he lives with the Cross in view. How does Paul identify with Christ in a way that you can apply to your life?

FRIENDS AND FAILURE

 Now on the first day of the week Mary Magdalene went to the tomb early, while it was still dark, and saw that the stone had been taken away from the tomb. Then she ran and came to Simon Peter, and to the other disciple, whom Jesus loved, and said to them, "They have taken away the Lord out of the tomb, and we do not know where they have laid Him." Peter therefore went out, and the other disciple, and were going to the tomb. So they both ran together, and the other disciple outran Peter and came to the tomb first. John 20:1-4 NKJV

WHO WERE the friends of Jesus? We immediately think of the disciples: Peter, Andrew, James, John, Philip, Bartholomew, Thomas, Matthew, James, Thaddaeus, Simon, and the false friend Judas. Although Jesus sent out seventy-two disciples in Luke 10:1, we don't get the impression that they were His close friends, certainly not like the Twelve. But who else was His friend? He had many followers and thrilled recipients of miracles; He had relatives, but what about friends?

The dictionary describes a friend as "one attached to another by affection or esteem." Friendship goes beyond acquaintance, or casually knowing another, because it implies commitment—being there in the rough times.

Jesus could have completed His work by Himself. But He chose to invest His time in relationships that were sometimes flawed and unreliable, just as He chooses to continue relationships with us today, relating as God and also as Friend.

A number of people in the Bible might have been friends with Jesus. John the Baptist was His cousin and also a loving friend for whom Jesus had high praise (Matthew 11:11). Jesus spent time at the homes of Simon the leper in Mark 14:3 and Zacchaeus (Luke 19:5). In Luke 8:2 several women traveled with Jesus and the disciples, including Mary Magdalene,

Joanna, and Susanna. They provided for Him from their own resources. Mary, the mother of James and Joseph, and Zebedee's wife, the mother of James and John, stayed with Him at the cross (Matthew 27:56; Mark 15:40) and later went to the tomb (Luke 24:1-8). Joseph of Arimathea and Nicodemus took care of Jesus' body after His death (Matthew 27:57-60; Mark 15:43-46; John 19:38-42).

Jesus didn't restrict His friendships to the upright and respected; He seemed to prefer those undervalued by society. He praised the sinful woman at the Pharisee's home who poured expensive perfume on His feet (Luke 7:37-38). And after the Resurrection, He first appeared to Mary Magdalene, from whom He had cast out seven demons (John 20:11-18). Mary, Martha, and Lazarus are mentioned frequently in the Gospels as people Jesus loved (Matthew 26:7; Luke 10:38-42; John 11 and 12).

In John 20, two friends who could have remained alienated got back together. Peter had denied the Lord and wept bitterly over this failure, while John had stayed at the foot of the cross and accepted the responsibility to care for Jesus' mother. But in John 20, they were reunited when faithful John reached out to Peter.

Perhaps true friendship is that which can withstand failure, the kind that can reach out in love to a fallen friend. That's what Jesus does for us every time we stumble and He extends a hand to bring us back to a right relationship with Him. He's the real Friend we all need.

What about You? Who are your close friends? Do they know how much you value them? Do they know that you accept them as they are, that there's room in your relationship for both failure and success?

Think of a friend who could use a word of encouragement and call that person today.

Take a Look In Luke 14:12-14 Jesus talked about humility and friendship. Think of one concrete way you can do what He urged in this passage the next time you have company.

THE BEST OF INTENTIONS

 Now Simon Peter stood and warmed himself. Therefore they said to him, "You are not also one of His disciples, are you?" He denied it and said, "I am not!" One of the servants of the high priest, a relative of him whose ear Peter cut off, said, "Did I not see you in the garden with Him?" Peter then denied again; and immediately a rooster crowed.
John 18:25-27 NKJV

YOU HAVE TO LOVE PETER. Headstrong and impetuous, he boldly declared his love for Jesus as he leaped to His defense in the Garden of Gethsemane. Peter was a passionate fellow who thought himself totally loyal to Christ. But a short time after the scene in the garden, Peter said three times that he didn't even know Jesus. Most of us can relate to his on-again, off-again courage. We are passionate about our love for God, but in a risky situation where speaking out for Him might cost us something in terms of ridicule, ostracism, or worse, we clam up just like Peter did.

Here Jesus is willingly giving Himself up because the time for His death has arrived, and Peter's brash action was not part of the plan. Jesus said to Peter in John 18:11 (NKJV), "Put your sword into the sheath. Shall I not drink the cup which My Father has given Me?" He knew the time had come to go to the Cross. The religious leaders, the soldiers, the crowd, and all Jesus' enemies thought they put Him to death, not knowing that the event had been planned from before the foundation of the world and that Jesus did it of His own volition.

But brave Peter wanted to protect his Lord in the garden. Imagine his grief later when the rooster crowed, reminding Peter of Jesus' prediction that Peter would deny Him three times. Matthew's account says that Peter "went out and wept bitterly" (Matthew 26:75 NKJV).

Linda could relate to Peter's situation. Her family had just moved in when she was invited to a neighborhood coffee. She gladly attended, eager to meet and get to know her new neighbors.

She was a little disturbed by the negative talk going on when she joined a group of about half a dozen women in the kitchen, but she just listened, knowing there are usually two sides to every story. But when a tall blonde woman turned to the woman next to her and said, "Did I tell you that my daughter is dating one of those Holy Rollers who is in church every waking moment?" Linda felt her face turn red. She and her husband were Christians, and they had begun to attend a church about ten minutes from their new home. She said nothing, wondering what would be said next.

"Not another one," was the reply. "Those people are so fanatical it really makes me wonder if they're normal. Remember that Christian family that used to live next door to me? They were really weird. I don't know what they did for fun because it sure wasn't anything we do for fun!"

The blonde turned to Linda and asked if she had ever known any of those "weird Christians." *I need to say I'm one and say how much my faith means to me,* Linda thought. But as she looked back at the laughing eyes across the table, she quietly said, "Not really," hating herself for her cowardice.

Like Peter, Linda loved God, but the situation had intimidated her into silence.

What about You? Think of a time when you denied Jesus, either by your words or actions. Was it the time someone asked you how to get to heaven and you mumbled something about not being sure? Or the day your neighbor attacked Christianity and you stood by silently? Or perhaps the time you had too much to drink at the company picnic?

Even before Peter denied knowing Him, Jesus said He had prayed for Peter, that his faith should not fail; "and when you have returned to Me, strengthen your brethren" (Luke 22:32 NKJV). He forgave Peter in advance and welcomed him to come back after Peter had denied knowing Him. We all blow it from time to time, missing chances to share our faith or honor God in our lives, but He is always there, always ready to take us back. Confess your sin and your missed opportunities to Him, and He will forgive you.

Take a Look Psalm 51:12 is David's prayer for a restoration of the joy of his salvation. Pray this verse back to God, asking Him to supply you with the strength to stand firm in your convictions and speak for Him when appropriate.

YOU WANT ME TO DO WHAT?

 He called out, "Friends, have you caught any fish?" "No," they replied. Then he said, "Throw out your net on the right-hand side of the boat, and you'll get plenty of fish!" So they did, and they couldn't draw in the net because there were so many fish in it. John 21:5-6

MARY KAY ASH, founder of the successful Mary Kay Cosmetics empire, began the business after retiring from a twenty-five-year sales career. When she started the business, she had very little money and three children to support as a single mom. But through hard work, persistence, and a goal of honoring God in her business, Mary Kay Cosmetics grew into an international business with billions of dollars in annual sales. It was my privilege to be her pastor and she was a faithful steward.

After her cosmetics company was established, Mary Kay was asked to speak in her church about the need to raise funds for an expansion. The fund-raising campaign had been going on for several months, with less than a thousand dollars coming in each week. Through a variety of circumstances, Mary Kay was unable to prepare properly for the talk, as she normally would have done. She arrived at church late and did not know what to say. She sensed God telling her to say she would match whatever amount was given for the project that day. She said that in her remarks and sat down, feeling silly.

That evening one of the church leaders called to thank her for her talk and for pledging to match whatever came in. He said, "We want you to know that we are not going to hold you to that offer in view of what's happened." Her hopes began to climb that maybe at least a thousand dollars had been pledged.

"Oh, no, I want to fulfill my promise," she said. "How much was pledged?"

"A little over $107,000!" Mary Kay was stunned and began to wonder how she would match such a huge amount. She decided to take a loan and repay it when she could. But the next day her son Richard, who was also the company's business manager and her personal financial advisor, called and said, "Mom, everything you touch seems to turn to gold. I don't know if you remember the two small investments we made in oil wells a couple of years ago, but they have come in and your share of the profits is one hundred thousand dollars!"

Mary Kay concluded correctly that you can't outgive God.

In John 21 the fishermen had had a bad night of fishing. In fact, they had caught nothing. Imagine their skepticism when Jesus said to lower the net once again.

Can't you hear them whine, "But, Lord . . ."? Nevertheless, they obeyed Him, with outstanding results.

We don't need to see the full net before we do what God tells us to do. In fact, that's when He does amazing things, when we can't see anything good ahead and we're about to give up.

Why not let down your net, trust God to fill it, and move out in faith, as Mary Kay did? You, too, will find God faithful. Jesus will never let you down.

What about You? Is God calling you to a step of obedience that seems too risky to take? Are you hesitating and holding back because you're not sure the plan will work?

Ask God to help you obey Him even when you don't see how He's going to provide for you. He'll surprise you with abundance.

Take a Look In Ephesians 3:20-21 Paul talks about how God exceeds our dreams and expectations. Read these verses and join him in giving "glory in the church and in Christ Jesus forever and ever through endless ages."

THE HEART OF GOD

 So when they had eaten breakfast, Jesus said to Simon Peter,
"Simon, son of Jonah, do you love Me more than these?" He
said to Him, "Yes, Lord; You know that I love You." He said
to him, "Feed My lambs." He said to him again a second time,
"Simon, son of Jonah, do you love Me?" He said to Him, "Yes,
Lord; You know that I love You." He said to him, "Tend My
sheep." John 21:15-16 NKJV

BEFORE HE ASKED, Jesus knew what Peter's feelings for Him
were. But He asked Peter if he loved Him in order to help Peter
move through his failure and toward success, and also to state
emphatically what He expects of all believers.

Jesus wants us to pour our lives into other people, as He
poured out His life for us. He had already told the disciples to
preach the Good News to all people. He had told them that love
should be their hallmark and He had told them what to expect
after He had gone to heaven.

But here He became very specific about what they were to do
next. They were to fill in for Him as shepherd of His sheep. In
the same way that shepherds meet all the needs of their flocks,
so the disciples were to meet the needs of Jesus' flock. By doing
so, they would show the sincerity of their love for Him.

Feeding the sheep includes more than just providing physical
food, but meeting physical needs is an important component.

Since 1867 in London, the Salvation Army—originally called
The Christian Mission—has been feeding the sheep by bringing
both the Good News of salvation and also humanitarian relief
to hurting people. Founder William Booth and his wife,
Catherine, traveled throughout England conducting evangelis-
tic meetings, and many of those who responded were the poor
and hungry. The first meeting in America was held in 1879 in
Philadelphia by Lieutenant Eliza Shirley.

The Salvation Army is dedicated to caring for the poor, feeding the hungry, clothing the naked, loving the unlovable, and befriending the friendless. It successfully combines social services with preaching the message of Christ. Its more than one hundred and twenty adult rehabilitation centers provide residential substance abuse care, including meals, shelter, medical services, work training, and spiritual guidance. The Army provides food and other necessities for disaster victims as well as housing for the poor and homeless, among many other services.

As an organization and as individual members of the Army, this group has taken Jesus' instructions to feed His sheep very seriously. They have put practicality to Jesus' genuine desire that the unfortunate should be cared for.

Jesus' desire that we care for others is clear. In 1 Timothy 6:17-19, Paul plainly states that the rich should use their money to do good and give generously to those in need since God has given their wealth to them.

Jesus' exhortation to care for His sheep was one of the last sayings of the book of John. Similarly, before He died on the cross, one of the last things Jesus did was to ask John to care for His mother. Here, as His time on earth draws to a close, the resurrected Christ once again looks out for the needs of His beloved followers when He says repeatedly, "Feed My sheep." Surely, caring for others' spiritual and physical needs was a true priority for Him.

Can it be anything less for us?

What about You? One day God will ask each of us, "What did you do with My Son Jesus Christ? What did you do with the life I've given you? Did you commit yourself to Jesus and follow Him?"

As you come to the end of the book of John, formulate your answer for the future date when you will be required to give it. If it's not the answer you would like to give, make the necessary changes today so that you can one day tell God that you followed Him with all your heart.

Take a Look   Read Luke 12:27-34 and find two promises about God's care for us.

SECTION **5**

Changer of My Heart

THE RIGHT REASONS

 Jesus looked around and saw them following. "What do you want?" he asked them. They replied, "Rabbi" (which means Teacher), "where are you staying?" "Come and see," he said. It was about four o'clock in the afternoon when they went with him to the place, and they stayed there the rest of the day. John 1:38-39

DAN CAME TO GOD in desperation. His wife had left him when she found out about his affair with one of his company's sales reps. His wife had taken their two daughters and moved in with her sister's family until she could decide what to do.

Not knowing where to turn, Dan called Kevin, a friend who had recently talked to Dan about Jesus. Kevin told Dan he had really messed things up.

"How can I get her back? What do I do?" Dan asked his friend.

Kevin told Dan that he didn't know how or if Dan could get his wife back, but he did know how Dan could be forgiven for his sins and become a new person. Kevin wasn't sure whether Dan really wanted to get to know God or just wanted God to fix his life. But he gave him several Bible verses and explained how to approach God in prayer. He knew if Dan truly wanted to be forgiven, God would take care of the rest.

Jesus always looks straight into our hearts, knowing our true motives and inviting us to follow Him. This ability to discern our thoughts and desires is what makes it easy for us to get close to Him.

In John 1:38-39, John the Baptist's disciples, Andrew and the author John, began to follow Jesus. We don't know whether they were really just curious to find out where He was staying or if they genuinely sought His leadership. They had come to Him purely on the testimony of John the Baptist.

People come to Christ for many different reasons. Some are seekers, some are skeptics, some are eager, some are rebellious. While on earth, Jesus treated each person differently, based on his or her needs. He didn't treat Nicodemus, the rabbi, the same way He dealt with the woman at the well. He tailored His conversation to meet each person's true needs. He knew their hearts and their motives. He knew their deepest longings and their deepest fears. When we come for the right reasons—honestly searching for God—He's only too glad to respond with His matchless love.

What about You? What are you looking for? What do you want from Jesus? Is it happiness? Security? Significance? Success? Do you go to church out of duty, or because of pressure from a family member? Or do you go seeking Jesus, desiring to know Him better? If so, He says to you, just as He did to Andrew and John, "Come and see." He turns to meet every person truly looking for Him. Come up close and get to know Him. Come just as you are, and ask Him all of your questions. And, like the disciples, stay with Him a while. He won't disappoint you.

Take a Look Jeremiah 33:3 (NKJV) says, "Call to Me, and I will answer you, and show you great and mighty things, which you do not know." Look up Romans 10:13 to find another promise for those who call on Him in genuine love.

DIAMONDS IN THE ROUGH

And he brought him to Jesus. Now when Jesus looked at him, He said, "You are Simon the son of Jonah. You shall be called Cephas" (which is translated, A Stone). John 1:42 NKJV

WHEN THEY WERE first found in India in 400 B.C., diamonds were believed to be splinters of stars. Kings and rulers wore them as charms to ward off evil spirits. The diamond is the hardest known natural material, so hard it could not be cut until the fourteenth century.

The stones are formed by a long, slow process of crystallization under intense heat and pressure in hot lava miles beneath the earth's surface. The diamonds are then carried to the surface of a volcano and later transported by rivers and streams to other locations. When uncut, diamonds are dull and uninteresting stones, but polished and shaped, they become priceless gems.

When Jesus, the ultimate Artist, met Peter, He saw the priceless gem beneath the surface of the uncut stone. Those who knew Peter might never have imagined the blustery, rugged fisherman as a follower of Christ. Peter was emotional, explosive, and rough, but his brother Andrew convinced him to come and meet the Messiah.

Jesus saw Peter's weaknesses, but He also saw his potential. He said Peter's given name (Simon) meant "listener" but from then on his name would be "the Rock," quite a nickname for someone who was unstable, insensitive, and weak. Jesus saw what Peter was that day, but in changing his name, He showed him what he would become.

Jesus sees the possibilities in you and me, too. In the same way that an artist such as Monet can take a nearly worthless piece of canvas and turn it into an invaluable treasure, Jesus can take the blank slate of our lives and create a priceless work of art. The value doesn't come from the canvas; it results from the name, the authentic signature of the one who did the work. We can become something very valuable, even a real diamond, because of Jesus' signature on our lives.

What about You? Can you see yourself as a masterpiece, made into a piece of art by Jesus' work? Are you thinking of your flaws and failures and wondering if those areas can possibly be fixed up, even by God? They can. He can make your life brand new. When He looks at you, He sees through all of your struggles to what you can become, what He longs to make of you.

Ask Him to polish and shape you into the priceless treasure He knows you can be.

Take a Look Read the story of Moses in Exodus 2–4. He was a man who had murdered a man, fled Egypt, and made excuses to God as to why he couldn't lead God's people to freedom. Yet God smoothed and shaped him into one of the great heroes of the faith mentioned in Hebrews 11.

List other Bible characters who were transformed from unlovely stone to useful treasure by the hand of God.

HOUSECLEANING

 Now when He was in Jerusalem at the Passover, during the feast, many believed in His name when they saw the signs which He did. But Jesus did not commit Himself to them, because He knew all men, and had no need that anyone should testify of man, for He knew what was in man.
John 2:23-25 NKJV

MY HOUSECLEANING methods are a bit unorthodox. I tend to save all sorts of things because, I tell myself, *You never know when you might need that piece of paper again.* In fact, I've even been known to go through the trash, pulling out things that my wife has thrown away. But occasionally, when my clutter has built to an intolerable level, I get rid of everything, rushing to clean out every last scrap. This is not an effective cleaning method, and it's not a good way to keep our lives clean either.

Just as Jesus cleaned out the Temple, He wants to clean out our lives as well. Instead of letting the clutter of sin pile up, we need to be honest and real with God day by day, confessing our sins and keeping our lives clean.

Of course, without God's power, we can't clean up our lives on our own. In Jesus' day, the people were expecting a military Messiah to deliver them from the power of Rome. They expected Him to upend the government, not the religious system. But Jesus started by dealing straightforwardly with the religious leaders and with the people of faith about the need for repentance. If the world is going to change today, it must begin with those who believe in Christ. It must begin with us.

Before we can change, we need God's light to illuminate the areas of our lives where we are blind or in denial. Jesus knows our hearts: "The human heart is most deceitful and desperately wicked" (Jeremiah 17:9). He saw that some of those following

Him believed only because they had seen His miracles, and He knew their shallow faith wouldn't last.

Most of us come to Jesus because we have a need that only He can fulfill. We are looking for the authentic miracle He can do in our lives. But after we come, we need to allow our faith to grow deeper than just our need, developing into a love relationship with Him. Part of that growth involves housecleaning, getting rid of the sinful clutter that dirties up our lives.

Once we've cleaned up and the clutter's gone at home, we can concentrate on those around us instead of feeling frazzled by the mess nearby. We can build our relationships undistracted by waiting untidiness. Similarly, once our spiritual house is clean and the distracting clutter of sin is gone, we can focus on Jesus, deepening our relationship with Him through prayer and listening to Him, worship, and Bible reading.

What about You? How does your spiritual house look right now? What does Jesus see in your heart? If He walked into your life as He walked into the Temple, what would He see that would anger Him and cause Him to turn it over and drive it out?

Ask Jesus to deepen your relationship with Him, to drive your roots down deep into His Word, to increase your faith and your willingness to obey and trust Him. A clean house is a more enjoyable place to live than a messy house. It provides a sense of calm, the comfort of orderliness, and a feeling of peace. Don't wait for Him to upend your life to get your attention. Let Him clean your life every day as you get to know Him more deeply.

Take a Look In Luke 11:39-41 Jesus said, "You Pharisees are so careful to clean the outside of the cup and the dish, but inside you are still filthy—full of greed and wickedness! Fools! Didn't God make the inside as well as the outside? So give to the needy what you greedily possess, and you will be clean all over."

List several ways a person can be clean or "religious" on the outside, but filthy on the inside.

YES, BUT . . .

For God did not send His Son into the world to condemn the world, but that the world through Him might be saved. He who believes in Him is not condemned; but he who does not believe is condemned already, because he has not believed in the name of the only begotten Son of God. John 3:17-18 NKJV

"I DON'T GO to church because the church is full of hypocrites." "If God were a God of love, He wouldn't let bad things happen, and He sure wouldn't send anyone to hell." "Sincere people in other religions are all on the road to heaven, too. Christianity is too exclusive." These statements are some of the most common reasons people give for rejecting Christianity.

Some who ask these questions are sincere skeptics who are honestly looking for answers. They don't understand, and they want to understand. But others use these objections as excuses to stay away from Jesus Christ and to justify unbelief.

How should Christians address these questions?

First we need to take a look at the objections. Are there hypocrites in the church? Yes, we're guilty as charged. Of course, there are hypocrites outside the church as well. But there are also wonderful people in the church, people who will love you sometimes even more than your family can love you. All Christians sin, but not all Christians are hypocrites who say one thing and do another.

The fact that there are sinners and hypocrites in the church doesn't lessen its credibility. Jesus didn't tell us to follow a Christian or a church or a pastor. He said, "Follow Me."

Second, how do you answer when someone asks how a God of love can let bad things happen? Many theories exist about God's role in our world. Some say that God created the world and then turned it loose to do what it would on its own. Others believe He set up His laws and can't break into the system to change it. Still others wonder if maybe He just doesn't have the power to stop the suffering.

The flaw in this line of thinking is that somehow we humans think we're in the position to pass moral judgment upon God, as if we are the moral center of the universe, deciding what's good or bad, what's right or wrong. If God doesn't do it our way, then He must be wrong. But when He created us, He gave each one of us the right to choose. He didn't want robots who would obey Him simply because we're programmed to do so. Think how hollow and empty the love of your spouse or child would be if he were forced to love you by some inner program beyond his control. God allowed us to choose, and we chose sin, ushering in the suffering that exists on earth today. God is in control, but He allows us to choose our own way, promising to bring good out of the worst situations. In fact, He often uses tragedy and suffering to show His love to hurting people, to draw them to Himself.

And it's important to note that God never sent anyone to hell. Jesus said hell is a place prepared for the devil and his angels, and He is not willing that any human being should go there. In 2 Peter 3:9 (NKJV) the Bible says, "[God is] not willing that any should perish but that all should come to repentance." If someone wants to know God, He promises to reveal Himself to that person.

A third criticism of Christianity is that it excludes other beliefs. Christians believe there is only one way to God, through the blood of Christ. We base that belief on Jesus' own words: "I am the way, the truth, and the life. No one comes to the Father except through Me" (John 14:6 NKJV). That statement leaves no room for other options. As Christians, we're called to deliver the message that Jesus gave us. But we must never use that message as justification for feeling superior to others. Often, it's not the message that's offensive, but the attitude with which we deliver it. A sincere study of world religions leads to the conclusion that they all believe different things about how a person is saved, who God is, what the Word of God is, and who Jesus Christ is. It also reveals the great need in this world for truth: the truth of an actual Savior, the very Son of God. What a privilege that we've been called to share such a truth!

What about You? Have you used one or more of the statements at the beginning of this devotion to stay away from God? If so, take Him at His word and ask Him to reveal Himself to you. "And you will seek Me and find Me, when you search for Me with all your heart" (Jeremiah 29:13 NKJV).

Take a Look James 4:8 (NKJV) says, "Draw near to God and He will draw near to you." List three ways you can come near to God, and do at least one of them today.

A SURE THING

 The official pleaded, "Lord, please come now before my little boy dies." Then Jesus told him, "Go back home. Your son will live!" And the man believed Jesus' word and started home.
John 4:49-50

JENNY WAS DESPERATE. A single mom with three young children, her child support check was a month late, her four-year-old son needed an antibiotic for strep throat, and her salary as a food service worker did not cover her family's basic needs.

She hated to call her dad again. He had just bailed her out two months ago when her car had broken down, and he had lent her the money for the repairs. But she knew his heart, how he loved her and his grandchildren, and she knew that he would be only too glad to help her. Again.

She made the call. Her dad agreed to bring over the money for the medicine when he got off work, so Jenny used the last of her grocery cash to purchase the antibiotic immediately, relieved that her dad would come through for her again.

She acted on her belief that her dad would help her. She didn't even wait to have his money in hand to act on her faith in her dad's commitment.

In the same way, the nobleman knew beyond a doubt that Jesus had the ability to heal his son. His belief led him to press on even after Jesus challenged him and the others present in verse 48, "Must I do miraculous signs and wonders before you people will believe in me?" Jesus knew they needed more than a miracle; they needed a Savior. He told them that faith is not what you see, feel, or think, but rather what you believe. In Hebrews, we see the true definition for faith: "Now faith is the substance of things hoped for, the evidence of things not seen" (Hebrews 11:1 NKJV).

The nobleman was probably so worried about his son's health that he gave little thought to his motivations. He just knew Jesus could help his son, and he asked. He surrendered to Christ and believed that He would do what He said He would do. He made the faith connection, taking Jesus at His word. And he obeyed Jesus and headed home. His faith grew as he learned what Jesus had done for him. He had an authentic encounter with Jesus.

Like Jenny and the nobleman, it's easy to feel that desperation when our need seems overwhelming. We find ourselves in financial difficulty and wonder where to turn. We know God can help us and has promised to provide, but fear and uncertainty threaten to send us into a state of panic. But if we act on our faith and hand over our problem to Him, daring to believe that He will help us, He will respond and build our faith through His answer. We must do our part—actively work to pay off debts, for example—relying on God to help us.

What about You? What's going on in your life where you need Jesus to intervene, where your resources and your accomplishments and your efforts just can't fix it? Is it a family member in crisis, a child dying, a marriage falling apart, a financial reversal? Will you trust Him to do what's best in the situation, to handle it much better than you can?

Ask for His help, take Him at His word, and obey Him. He'll take care of it for you. It may not be a miraculous healing—or it may be—but it will be what is best in the big picture of eternity for you and your loved ones.

Take a Look Jesus offers to carry our load of problems, no matter how heavy they are. "Come to me, all of you who are weary and carry heavy burdens, and I will give you rest" (Matthew 11:28). Rest sounds good, doesn't it? "Now I can rest again, for the LORD has been so good to me" (Psalm 116:7). Meditate on these two verses about the rest Jesus wants to provide.

TOUGH ASSIGNMENTS

 Then Jesus lifted up His eyes, and seeing a great multitude coming toward Him, He said to Philip, "Where shall we buy bread, that these may eat?" But this He said to test him, for He Himself knew what He would do. Philip answered Him, "Two hundred denarii worth of bread is not sufficient for them, that every one of them may have a little."
John 6:5-7 NKJV

EXAMS ARE part of teaching and learning. The teacher gives the material to the students, the students study, and the teacher tests their knowledge with an exam. While we know that God doesn't test anyone in the sense of tempting him or her to sin (James 1:13), He does help us learn by giving us exams from time to time.

He tested Philip by asking a question, not because Jesus didn't know the answer, but because He wanted to help Philip grow in his faith. It is likely that Philip was from the surrounding area and would be familiar with nearby sources of food. He had been looking around at the crowd, estimating the number of people and what it would cost to feed them. His estimate of two hundred denarii was the equivalent of a working man's wages for an entire year. But Philip's calculation was based on human resources, not on Jesus' resources. He had seen Jesus do some amazing feats, but when he calculated the cost of the food he forgot to factor in faith; he neglected to include Jesus in his figures.

Most of us are like Philip when faced with a test. We immediately try to think of how to solve the situation ourselves. We get busy evaluating and calculating, all without going to God for His help and His power. We pick up the phone and call someone for help, forgetting that the greatest help is but a whisper away.

But, like Philip, when we figure without Christ in the picture, we don't arrive at the best answer. We may solve the problem or escape from the hard situation, but we haven't maximized the good we can get from difficulty. God tests us so that our faith will grow. He challenges us in order to strengthen and mature us. Without tests or problems, we wouldn't know that God is able to solve them. James 1:2-4 says, "Dear brothers and sisters, whenever trouble comes your way, let it be an opportunity for joy. For when your faith is tested, your endurance has a chance to grow. So let it grow, for when your endurance is fully developed, you will be strong in character and ready for anything." It's very hard to welcome problems because no one wants them, but remembering that they can be used for good can help make them bearable.

Notice how Abraham passed his great test in Genesis 22:9-12. For Abraham, everything was at risk. God was commanding him to sacrifice the life of his beloved and long-awaited son. Yet Abraham didn't scurry around trying to find an alternative sacrifice that might please God. He didn't beg or plead or plot how he could take Isaac and Sarah and run away to another country and avoid obedience. He passed the test, and his faith and obedience were rewarded greatly. God used the test to strengthen Abraham.

When Job was tested, he cried out and asked God many questions. He even despaired of life itself. But his faith was strengthened and refined when God showed Job who He was. That's what we can all see in a test—who God is and what He can do.

In John 6 Jesus provided actual food to meet the actual need of the crowd that day. He promises to provide for your real needs as well.

What about You? Are you in the middle of a difficult exam today, wondering if you're going to pass or fail the test? The surest way to pass is to immediately ask God to come alongside you and use His power to help you.

SECTION 5: CHANGER OF MY HEART

Take a Look   Read Psalm 139:23 where David asked God to test him and know his thoughts. Can you think of a time or times in David's life when God did reveal the condition of David's heart to him?

FAMINE OF THE SOUL

 But you shouldn't be so concerned about perishable things like food. Spend your energy seeking the eternal life that I, the Son of Man, can give you. For God the Father has sent me for that very purpose. John 6:27

THE CROWDS WANTED a show. They wanted Jesus to perform and to amaze them with more miracles. They came to Him for many reasons. Some wanted a political king to overthrow Rome, a king they could control. Some came for emotional reasons, desiring another thrill. They didn't realize that what they really needed was Jesus Himself in their lives. They didn't recognize their spiritual hunger, the same hunger every person has.

We feel physical hunger in the body. Prolonged hunger can be seen in the swollen bellies, balding heads, and protruding joints of famine victims. And spiritual hunger can be felt, too, in hopelessness, dread, and despair. It manifests itself as emptiness and lack of purpose.

In the same way that eating a substance that isn't really food, like sand or pebbles, wouldn't provide necessary nourishment, feeding spiritual hunger with frenetic activity, or money and possessions, or addictive behaviors won't satisfy your spiritual need either. Only the real thing—real food or the real Jesus—can provide the nourishment we need. He is totally God, yet totally man, the great I Am, the only one who can truly satisfy our deepest needs and longings.

Along with the physical drive for food, human beings have a strong drive to acquire knowledge and to achieve. A look at life a hundred years ago, with horses and buggies as the main mode of transportation, is a reminder that life has changed. People naturally search for meaning in life and wonder about the eternal questions such as, *Why am I here? Where am I going?* The Greek word for man is *anthropos,* meaning the "upward looking one," unlike animals who are focused upon the earth, looking down. God created us with a capacity to look up and beyond ourselves and the things of earth, and to know Him. He created us with a spiritual hunger, a deep inner desire to know Him.

Disillusionment and emptiness are widespread today. Many have turned to Eastern religions and mysticism because of broken relationships, fractured families, financial catastrophes, illness, and a host of other problems. Some have committed suicide.

These people are empty because they have the same basic need that's in the heart of every person—to know God and experience His presence and power. Jesus came to reveal God so that we don't have to be empty and spiritually starved. While He did miracles and preached eloquently, He wasn't really here for the show. He was here to feed souls as only He can do, with the genuine spiritual food only He can provide.

What about You? Are you hungry, or empty, or disillusioned, or discouraged? Like the woman at the well and the nobleman with a sick son and the crippled woman who encountered Jesus, you, too, can be filled and satisfied with the life only available in Jesus Christ.

Take a Look Read about the good plans God has for you in Jeremiah 29:11. Write in your words what kind of plan this verse says God has for you and your life.

HARD WORDS

 Therefore many of His disciples, when they heard this, said, "This is a hard saying; who can understand it?" When Jesus knew in Himself that His disciples complained about this, He said to them, "Does this offend you? What then if you should see the Son of Man ascend where He was before? It is the Spirit who gives life; the flesh profits nothing. The words that I speak to you are spirit, and they are life. But there are some of you who do not believe." For Jesus knew from the beginning who they were who did not believe, and who would betray Him. John 6:60-64 NKJV

"YOU'RE OUT." "Good-bye." "We're downsizing and your position no longer exists." "Your test was positive." Hard words to hear. Words that can change your life. Words that can break your heart.

Hard words are difficult both to deliver and to receive. The policeman who comes to the door to inform parents there has been a car accident in which their teen was involved carries a heavy burden—but not as heavy as that of the parents who will receive the news of the tragedy.

While Jesus was filled with compassion, at times he used hard words. Whether He was talking to the Pharisees or His own disciples, He spoke truth—truth that sometimes drove His listeners away.

For a while, the crowds stayed with Him, enjoying a free lunch and the entertainment of miracles. But when He called them to the challenging aspects of following Him, many dropped from sight. When He spoke about commitment and obedience, the thrill-seekers lost interest.

What were the difficult truths Jesus was talking about? First, He was saying that He is God. When He said He was the Bread of Life (John 6:35), He was making a claim to deity, to being

God. The living Bread of God was the Messiah, the Savior. And He said He came down from heaven (6:38), another reference to deity. These claims ignited the hostility of His listeners, and many walked away when He claimed to be God.

The fact that Jesus is God is a divisive truth today as well. When we say that there is only one name given among men whereby we must be saved, the name of Jesus (Acts 4:12), people are put off by the exclusivity of that claim. It's usually acceptable to talk about God, but when you talk about Jesus and who He is, people get upset.

The second tough truth Jesus talked about was the teaching concerning His death. In John 6:53 He spoke of eating His flesh and drinking His blood, not a literal eating and drinking, but rather the offering of His life as a sacrifice. When He began to speak of dying for the sins of the world, people were repulsed. They wanted the Messiah to come and rule as king, not to die a horrible death.

The same reactions occur today. When you say that the death of Christ paid for the sins of the world so that each person can be forgiven, some people become uncomfortable. They don't mind talking about Christ as a moral teacher, a rabbi, a great man, or a prophet. But when you talk about blood, even the precious blood of Jesus that cleanses us from sin, people get upset.

It's hard to admit we're sinners who can't save ourselves. It goes against the pride, arrogance, and ego of our culture, which says we can do everything for ourselves. But the Bible says that without the shedding of blood, there's no remission of sin (Hebrews 9:22).

What about You? What's your response to the hard teachings of Jesus? Are you repulsed or attracted? Defensive or thankful? Can you admit that no matter how self-sufficient and successful you might be in many areas of life, you can do nothing about the condition of your heart, about the sins that keep finding their way back into your life despite your good intentions?

222

SECTION 5: CHANGER OF MY HEART

These teachings are challenging, but they're also life-giving and freeing. The God who created us sent His Son to die for us and pave the way to new and vibrant living.

Take a Look Sometimes hard words need to be said. But in Psalm 19:14 we find a reminder about all the words we say: "May the words of my mouth and the thoughts of my heart be pleasing to you, O Lord, my rock and my redeemer."

THE RIVER OF LIFE

 On the last day, that great day of the feast, Jesus stood and cried out, saying, "If anyone thirsts, let him come to Me and drink. He who believes in Me, as the Scripture has said, out of his heart will flow rivers of living water." John 7:37-38 NKJV

WHAT COMES to your mind when you think of a river?

Mark Twain depicted the excitement of river adventures in his classic tales of Tom Sawyer and Huckleberry Finn. Henry David Thoreau said, "[Rivers] are the constant lure, when they flow by our doors, to distant enterprise and adventure." The river is often used as a metaphor for life, as we meander this way and that, collecting and releasing bits and pieces along the way, until we reach our ultimate destination.

Rivers accomplish much. Up in the mountains, snow melts and mountain streams travel downward, carving out valleys, creating waterfalls, and merging with other nearby streams. Eventually these combining streams get bigger and form a river.

In the life of the believer, the Living Water revitalizes and restores us as we experience the peaks and valleys everyone travels. It also washes out sediment as we repent and discard our sin along the way. It provides a constant source of refreshment for our souls and overflows from our lives into the lives of others.

Eventually, all rivers make their way toward a larger body of water, where the river splits into many channels, depositing silt and sediment, before pouring into the ocean. In the process, the river creates a habitat, a place for living communities.

As we have Jesus—the authentic Living Water—running through our hearts, we, too, can create places suitable for living communities (groups sharing common characteristics), places where others can come, experience love and acceptance, and get to know the Jesus who makes our lives possible. We can provide places of real refreshment for others.

Jesus doesn't say that this promise is just for pastors or missionaries or supersaints. Whether you are a student, a businessperson, or a parent, the Living Water flowing from your heart can transform you and those around you. You can be a river of refreshment to others as your countenance, your cheerfulness, and your hope invigorate and encourage those around you.

A. B. Senton said, "Not many rivers flow right into the ocean. Most rivers end up running into other rivers and the best workers are . . . content to empty their streams of blessing into other rivers."

What about You? Is your life a source of refreshment to those around you? Are you willing to pour yourself into others' lives without needing to get credit and commendation for what you do? Or would others describe your water as stagnant and polluted?

As believers, Jesus said we should refresh and restore others. Ask Him to flood your heart with His own living water.

Take a Look Read Psalm 1 and find several ways a righteous life is like a tree along a riverbank.

VITAL SIGNS

But this He spoke concerning the Spirit, whom those believing in Him would receive; for the Holy Spirit was not yet given, because Jesus was not yet glorified.   John 7:39 NKJV

THE TWO PARAMEDICS bent over Beth's husband, Aaron, after carefully extracting him from the driver's side of the car. The van that ran the red light had hit Aaron's side of the car. Beth's face was bleeding because, despite her seat belt, her head had banged into the windshield. But at least she was conscious. The paramedics asked her to stay where she was until they could stabilize Aaron. Beth studied her husband's pale face, and prayed that he would live.

But twenty minutes later, when they lifted the stretcher with Aaron on it into the ambulance and walked to where Beth still sat in the front seat, one of the men said, "We're not getting a pulse or blood pressure reading. We're taking him to the hospital."

Beth's heart sank as she heard that her husband's body lacked the vital signs of life. As she held Aaron's hand in the ambulance on the ride to the hospital, two paramedics worked on him, providing oxygen and starting an IV. When the ambulance came to a stop outside the emergency room, one of the men said, "I'm getting a slow pulse. Let's get him inside." Beth continued to pray with renewed hope that her husband might survive.

As Christians filled with the Spirit of God, we should show signs of His life in us. Before Jesus' death, believers did not have the Holy Spirit. In John 7:39 Jesus had not yet died on the cross, which is what the word *glorified* refers to, a glorious event because our salvation was completed by His death and resurrection. Here Jesus told the disciples that after He was gone His

Spirit would remain with them. On the day of Pentecost, recorded in Acts 2, the Spirit of God descended on the believers, and He now comes to each person at the moment he or she makes a commitment to Christ.

But how can we tell if someone is a believer? What are the vital signs of a genuine Spirit-filled life?

First, the Spirit-filled life is an obedient life marked by a desire to please God, a desire to know Him more and become more like Him. That means living like Christ in the presence of our families and in the presence of our coworkers. It's a life marked by humble thankfulness and by generosity. The Spirit of Christ is the spirit of grace, of sacrifice on behalf of others.

Second, the Spirit-filled life is an overflowing life, a life of fullness. God's Spirit overflows from us to others through love, and to God through praise and worship.

Third, the Spirit-filled life is an overcoming life. We have the ability to overcome the power of sin, to say no to temptation. According to Matthew 4, Jesus was full of the Spirit of God when He dealt with Satan. With the Word of God in His heart and His mind as the Son of God, He used the same resource we have to defeat the enemy. He wielded the sword of the Spirit, which is the Word of God (Ephesians 6:17). We can face life's battles with the Spirit enabling, protecting, and defending us.

How does the Spirit come into our lives? Paul said in his letter to the Galatians, "I have been crucified with Christ; it is no longer I who live, but Christ lives in me" (Galatians 2:20 NKJV). When we give our lives to Christ, His Spirit lives in us. But we can block His activity in our lives by sinning or by failing to give Him the freedom to do all that He wants to do.

We're full of the Holy Spirit when Jesus is in charge of our lives. It's not a question of getting more of the Spirit, but allowing the Spirit to have more of us. If we're already full—full of selfish pursuits and ambitions—there is no room for the Spirit. But when we give all that we are and have to Him, the Spirit of God can move with His pure and unadulterated power in our lives. We don't do good works by our own efforts: "'Not by might nor by power, but by My spirit,' says the LORD of hosts" (Zechariah 4:6 NKJV).

The vital signs of life in Christ prove that our faith is real.

What about You? Does your life display the vital signs of life in Christ? Do you have the Holy Spirit living in you because you trusted Jesus Christ as your Savior? If you do, are you allowing Him to have His way in your life?

Ask the Holy Spirit to fill you on a daily basis, to control you day by day. Ask Him to bring to your attention areas of your life that are not pleasing to God and help you change them. Ask for opportunities to overflow with His love to others every day.

Take a Look Look up Romans 8:27; 2 Corinthians 3:6; James 4:5-6; and 1 John 5:6-7. List four actions God's Spirit takes in our lives.

OUT OF THE DARKNESS

 He who follows Me shall not walk in darkness, but have the light of life. John 8:12 NKJV

I WAS A CHILD shopping downtown with my parents when I first saw him. We were at Everybody's, the less expensive version of Leonard Brothers department store across the street. I had never seen a beggar before, and the sightless man held a cup in one hand and a small sign in the other that read, "The sun is shining but I cannot see."

I tried to imagine what it would be like to be blind, to go through life in darkness, but I could not. Every time I tried to walk with my eyes closed, I automatically opened them as soon as I bumped into something. I knew that blindness must be a frightening experience.

Many people today have the physical sense of sight, but they do not see the important things of the spiritual realm. They walk around in darkness because they do not recognize Jesus Christ. They may attend church, listen to the sermon, sing the songs, and shake hands with others, but they just don't get it. They don't see with the eyes of faith because only the Holy Spirit can open eyes to the truth of Christ. If we take even the tiniest, most feeble and timid step of faith toward God He will begin to dispel the darkness and enable us to see.

Others live in darkness because they have rejected Christ outright. Satan has blinded their minds and they turn away from Jesus, refusing to believe in Him. But once our eyes are opened to Jesus, life takes on new meaning. Instead of seeing only the problems, the tragedies, the difficulties of life, we see that life also contains beauty and fulfillment. We know the meaning of the line in the poem *Desiderata* that says, "It is still a beautiful world."

Believers, too, can be blind in certain areas. Their hearts can be hardened to their sin so that they don't realize that the poisonous dart of gossip can do enormous harm, or that their caustic words to their wife or child cut deep. Sin loves the darkness, and it tries to stay hidden away out of our spiritual sight.

We can be blinded by untruth, by false doctrine, or by false teachers. We fail to scrutinize teaching by comparing it to the Bible and insisting on the genuine rather than the fake.

But Jesus says here that He is able to blow away the darkness and light our lives once and for all. That doesn't mean that He won't continue to reveal the hidden recesses of our minds that need to be dealt with in confession and repentance, but we will never again have to walk in the dark.

What about You? How is your spiritual sight? Is the light of Christ shining forth from you in your daily activities and words? Does the Holy Spirit have access to the dark regions of your mind and the freedom to expose them so you can be free? Do you shine the light of God's Word on the teaching you receive to see if it holds true?

Ask Jesus to chase away the darkness, to give you full sight in all areas, so that you may be productive for Him, living in and spreading His light.

Take a Look Look up Deuteronomy 16:19; Isaiah 56:10; and 2 Corinthians 4:4. List three results of spiritual blindness.

BELIEVING IS SEEING

So they again called the man who was blind, and said to him, "Give God the glory! We know that this Man is a sinner." He answered and said, "Whether He is a sinner or not I do not know. One thing I know: that though I was blind, now I see."
John 9:24-25 NKJV

DIANE WOULD HAVE none of Andrea's "God talk." She told her friend, "If it works for you, that's fine. But I haven't seen anything in the Bible that convinces me it's true."

"Have you read the Bible, Diane?" Andrea asked.

"Parts of it. And all I see is violence and war and killing. I don't need to read the rest to know it's not for me."

Andrea tried to tell Diane about all the prophecies about Jesus Christ that have come true, as well as prophecies about the nation of Israel. She pointed to nature and the magnificent, intricate structures of trees, birds, flowers, and the human body. Diane skipped over Andrea's comment about prophecies and said evolution explains nature and how it works.

Finally Andrea said, "Diane, the only way to really know whether the Bible is true and Jesus Christ is real is to get to know Him for yourself. Since I've given my life to Him, I've seen Him acting in my life and in my heart. Once you know Him, you see the reality of Jesus for yourself in a way that no one could ever adequately explain." Diane shrugged, unconvinced.

The religious leaders in this story were similarly unconvinced as they questioned the formerly blind man. He didn't know much about Jesus yet; he only knew that Jesus had changed his life for the better. He didn't understand theology the way the rabbis did. But he simply said what every Christian can say: "I know what Jesus has done in my life. I may not have everything figured out. I don't have all the answers, but I know He has touched me and changed my life."

The tiny seed of faith that this man exercised when he obeyed Jesus by washing himself in the pool of Siloam was all he needed to get to know the Savior. But his small faith sprouted quickly when he experienced Jesus' authentic love. He confounded the religious leaders when, in the initial stages of his salvation, he shared what Jesus had done in his life, his experience with Jesus.

He even had the courage to defend Jesus to his accusers: "Now we know that God does not hear sinners; but if anyone is a worshiper of God and does His will, He hears him. Since the world began it has been unheard of that anyone opened the eyes of one who was born blind. If this Man were not from God, He could do nothing" (John 9:31-33 NKJV). And for this statement, he was expelled from the Temple.

Always compassionate, when Jesus heard what had happened to the man, He went looking for him. When He asked if the man believed in the Son of God (verse 35), the man asked, "Who is He, Lord, that I may believe in Him?" (verse 36). When Jesus said it was He, his seedling faith blossomed. "'Lord, I believe!' And he worshiped Him" (verse 38).

This story paints a picture of how faith grows. It doesn't start with massive amounts of religious facts or information about God like the Pharisees possessed. It starts with hope and even the slightest willingness to take a step toward the One you believe to be true. The blind man fervently hoped that Jesus could and would help him, even though he didn't know who He was. His need propelled him to the Savior.

And then Jesus did the rest. He changed the man's life, bringing him face-to-face with the Son of God. The natural response was belief and worship of the true God.

What about You? What's the size of your faith today? Is it a tiny seed, a tender sapling, or a full-grown tree? Or is it a tree that's been blown around and weakened by the storms of life?

SECTION 5: CHANGER OF MY HEART

You can grow or strengthen your faith by following the blind-since-birth man's example. Allow your need to drive you to Jesus. Take a small step of faith toward Him by obeying what you read in the Bible. He will meet you and surprise you as you experience His touch on your life.

Then try sharing your faith—whatever its size—with someone else. Take the risk of defending Jesus to a skeptic. Study Him in the Bible and as you do, you'll come face-to-face with the Savior. You'll want to respond in worship.

Take a Look Write down the definition of faith given in Hebrews 11:1. Then read Matthew 21:19-22 to see how Jesus said to exercise and strengthen one's faith.

THE CHALLENGE OF CHANGE

 I will not leave you orphans; I will come to you. A little while longer and the world will see Me no more, but you will see Me. Because I live, you will live also. At that day you will know that I am in My Father, and you in Me, and I in you. He who has My commandments and keeps them, it is he who loves Me. And he who loves Me will be loved by My Father, and I will love him and manifest Myself to him.
John 14:18-21 NKJV

LIFE TODAY IS pretty stressful for most of us. Stressors are ranked according to how much stress a particular event places on an individual. Research has found that positive as well as negative events can cause stress because they often involve change that can be difficult to adapt to. Some common stressors and their ranks follow:

- *Death of a spouse* 100 points
- *Divorce* 73 points
- *Marriage* 50 points
- *Loss of job* 47 points
- *Pregnancy* 40 points
- *Buying a house* 31 points
- *Christmas* 12 points

Russ and Julie had three children, and the youngest had leukemia. One parent spent the night at the children's hospital with Amanda during each of her treatments. Finally, two years after her diagnosis, the doctors said she was in remission. Russ, Julie, and their extended family rejoiced and thanked God, knowing that the battle wasn't over, but at least there was a respite from the treatments that had made their daughter bald, but better.

A month after Amanda's last treatment Julie's seventy-three-year-old mother died suddenly and unexpectedly, leaving behind a complicated estate that took Julie, as executrix, many frustrating hours to handle. Julie was thankful that Amanda was in remission and that her treatments had been over by the time her mother died.

But when Julie's brother and his wife divorced after twenty-two years of marriage, Julie became deeply discouraged and depressed. She found it difficult to get through each day's tasks, and she asked God to help her.

Six months later when Russ lost his job, Julie collapsed emotionally, and went to her doctor. He said the stresses she had experienced would take a heavy toll on anyone and he referred her to a therapist.

In John 14:18-21 Jesus promises not to leave us alone in this stressful world. He promises that He will love us and show Himself to us. We don't have to face life's problems and changes by ourselves.

In Proverbs 3:5-6 (NKJV), we read, "Trust in the LORD with all your heart, and lean not on your own understanding; in all your ways acknowledge Him, and He shall direct your paths."

After all that she had encountered, Julie had a deeper understanding of God's promises. She thanked God for directing her steps toward someone who could help her. As He promised, Jesus didn't leave her alone in her darkest hour; He provided help, and His presence calmed her even though her stress score was off the charts. The reality of Jesus in her life held her together when she felt like flying apart.

Julie began counseling, and she also began journaling. She recorded her feelings and the sources of her stress in her journal as she took each concern to God every day. She also decided to turn each worry into a prayer prompt where every time a worry entered her mind, she would immediately pray about it. She began to list what she was thankful for and deliberately spent time each day going over that list and thanking God for each item on her list. When God helped her handle a negative feeling or answered a prayer, she noted it next to the journal entry where she had listed that feeling or stressor.

Although Julie's problems did not all go away, her perspective changed from looking at her life through eyes of gloom to counting her blessings. She found that God was strengthening her to handle her difficulties with peace instead of panic.

What about You? What is your current stress level? Have you experienced difficult events or positive events that involved change in the last year? How do you cope with stress?

Make a list of the stressors in your life. Take the list to Jesus in prayer and ask Him to show you how to handle them. Ask Him to make your path straight when it looks tangled. Remember that He promised to guide us if we ask.

Take a Look David knew all about stress. Some—not all—he brought on himself. He experienced emotional pits of despair. Read Psalm 13 where you'll see that David understood despair, but he also understood that God was listening and would always help him. How did David respond to stress and trouble?

HAPPY OR WHOLE

 These things I have spoken to you, that My joy may remain in you, and that your joy may be full. John 15:11 NKJV

WE ALL WANT to be happy, don't we? We want our children to be happy, our grandchildren to be happy, and our friends to be happy. But the trouble with happiness is that it depends on one's circumstances. If bad things happen, happiness evaporates. Or when the entertainment ends and work begins, we lose our happiness. Or when our health fails, it's hard to be happy about that.

Author F. Scott Peck, in his book *The Road Less Traveled,* begins with the unwelcome statement, "Life is difficult." His premise is that if we accept that fact, we will actually have a happier life than the person who expects life to be happy and is constantly disappointed when it isn't. He urges us to embrace difficulty and learn from it.

God cares more about our character than our happiness. Of course, He gives us all good things to enjoy (1 Timothy 6:17); He has a good plan to give us a future and a hope (Jeremiah 29:11), He works all things together for good to those who are called according to His purpose (Romans 8:28). But He doesn't just smooth out all of our circumstances so that we can glide along in life happy. He knows that, even though we'd rather avoid them, difficulty and even suffering can improve us, grow us, mature us, and make us more like the genuine Jesus, who understands suffering well.

That's why Jesus gives us His joy, so that when a sudden disaster occurs and happiness flits away, His joy, the deep inner sense that God is with us, remains. God knew we would need it because Nehemiah 8:10 says, "the joy of the LORD is your strength!" We need the strength that endures when happiness melts away with a falling stock market, or a death in the family, or a job loss.

In James 1:2-4 (NKJV), we read, "Count it all joy when you fall into various trials, knowing that the testing of your faith produces patience. But let patience have its perfect work, that you may be perfect and complete, lacking nothing."

God certainly doesn't orchestrate disaster in our lives, but He doesn't always prevent it either, even though He could. He knows that through trials, we will gain treasures worth much more than mere happiness—treasures such as patience and spiritual wholeness so that we lack nothing.

A wise parent doesn't make life too easy for his child because he wants the child to develop character, a solid work ethic, and responsibility. Likewise, God allows difficulties that can provide us with lasting riches, traits that only develop over time and often through struggle. And He promises that we won't have to go the tough road alone. The writer of Hebrews says, "He Himself has said, 'I will never leave you nor forsake you'" (Hebrews 13:5 NKJV).

Happiness is fleeting since it's tied to circumstances. Far better for us to obtain the lasting qualities of faith, hope, and perseverance that we develop to take with us into any and all circumstances.

What about You? Do you experience the lasting qualities of patience, perseverance, and joy even when your circumstances take a nosedive? Do you accept difficulty as a part of life, or do you really believe that life shouldn't be this way: it should get easier and happier?

Jesus promised us joy, not happiness; character, not ease. Ask God to help you grapple with difficulty in such a way that you grow in the valuable character traits that will help you throughout your life.

Take a Look Read Romans 5:3-5 for a further look at the benefits to be gained through trouble.

DISUNITED WE FALL

 I do not pray for these alone, but also for those who will believe in Me through their word; that they all may be one, as You, Father, are in Me, and I in You; that they also may be one in Us, that the world may believe that You sent Me.
John 17:20-21 NKJV

JUST AS A DEVASTATING FIRE can be started with the careless toss of a two-inch-long match, trouble among people can start with a very small beginning.

Amy loved old hymns and gospel songs, and while she also liked praise choruses and accompaniment by guitars and drums, it seemed to her like every Sunday there were more praise songs, louder drums, and fewer hymns.

As she left the service one beautiful fall morning, she said to her husband, Warren, "I'm really tired of the music in this church. I'm going to call Paul tomorrow morning and ask why we never sing any hymns anymore." Paul had been serving as the church's worship leader for just over a year.

Warren said, "We sang 'Great Is Thy Faithfulness' this morning, Amy. The contemporary service seems to be attracting a lot of new families, and we still have our concert series tickets where we can enjoy the classics. I don't mind the new worship style at all, but if you do, it's probably a good idea to go ahead and talk to Paul about it."

Amy wanted to have a good attitude, but the music issue bothered her for the remainder of the day, and Monday morning she called Paul at the church. His assistant said Monday was his day off and she would take a message.

By Thursday, Amy's call had not been returned, and she was angry. When her daughter's Sunday school teacher called and asked if Amy could substitute in the class on Sunday, Amy said,

"Sure, I'd rather not be in church anyway since I can't even get a call returned from one of our pastors." When Beth asked what she meant, Amy told her it seemed as though Paul was so set on doing things his own way that he didn't even bother to return phone calls. Beth repeated Amy's complaint to a friend who was teetering on the brink of leaving the worship team because of scheduling difficulties. This friend decided to quit the team if its leader was the type of person who didn't even return phone calls.

Within a month, gossip and innuendo had circulated among a number of worship team members who then began to come late or skip practice altogether, using as an excuse the obviously low degree of commitment on the part of their leader who didn't return calls.

Kenneth had joined the worship team three months earlier. He and his son had been in the United States for only two years, having fled Sudan's turmoil. Their church had been burned to the ground by rebels who opposed religion after famine had decimated the church's families. Kenneth was puzzled by the talk about Paul, and when he finally understood why people were quitting the worship team, he left the church, heart-broken. The church had so much to be thankful for, and yet they were destroying themselves. He couldn't continue to be a part of the painful situation.

Many smaller—and larger—issues than music style can divide churches. Complaints and criticism seem to grow like yeast in dough, taking on larger proportions over a short period of time, especially if the heat of gossip is applied.

While many of these squabbles are petty, Jesus foresaw how easy it would be for believers to become divided on even insignificant matters. In this prayer, He asked that believers who respond in faith to the disciples' teaching would be united as Jesus and His Father are united; He implied that lack of unity could prevent others from believing in God. He asks that we would be one "that the world may believe that You sent Me."

Where fighting and discord replace unity, what will attract non-believers to the church? Where is the genuine love that Jesus said will be the mark of His followers?

Throughout church history, various factions have battled for supremacy or have fought to be "right." While the tenets of the faith—such as biblical inerrancy and the deity of Christ—must always be defended and upheld, many other divisions could be healed by agreeing to disagree or by forgiveness. Areas like worship style, clothing choices, personal habits, and others that are not clearly delineated in the Bible are not worth fighting over.

Jesus asked God to give us unity as believers, unity based on the truth of who He is in the Bible. We must put away "bitterness, wrath, anger, clamor, and evil speaking . . . with all malice. And be kind to one another, tenderhearted, forgiving one another, even as God in Christ forgave you" (Ephesians 4:31-32 NKJV). Only then can we help put out the fires of gossip and criticism that are so very damaging and enjoy the true unity God desires for us.

What about You? How do you handle gossip? Do you listen or do you refuse even to be a part of it in that way? When you have a grievance, do you go directly to the person involved or do you tell someone else about it first?

Why not take steps today to reconcile with those against whom you have a complaint, either offering or asking for forgiveness?

Take a Look Read Matthew 18:15-35 and outline the steps we should take when we have a grievance against another believer.

PASSING THE BUCK

 Pilate then went out to them and said, "What accusation do you bring against this Man?" They answered and said to him, "If He were not an evildoer, we would not have delivered Him up to you." Then Pilate said to them, "You take Him and judge Him according to your law." Therefore the Jews said to him, "It is not lawful for us to put anyone to death," that the saying of Jesus might be fulfilled which He spoke, signifying by what death He would die. John 18:29-32 NKJV

JUSTIN QUIT HIS JOB in disgust. This was the third job he had quit since leaving college two years ago at the age of twenty. At all three jobs, his supervisor had been a jerk, too demanding and incompetent in Justin's view. When the last boss had complained that Justin had come in a half hour late twice in one week, Justin quit because he didn't want a boss who picked on him all the time.

He had left college because the teachers were bad. They, too, picked on him and made his life difficult. When he skipped exams and failed courses, Justin got angry. The teachers could have easily let him make up the tests on another day when he felt better.

Justin's situation may sound extreme, but he's not alone. Many people today avoid taking personal responsibility and blame others for their problems. Buck-passing cuts across all age and economic groups. Corporate leaders say the accountants or consultants made the mistakes that led to false reporting, and the accountants and consultants say they only work with the numbers the executives provide.

But buck-passing goes back a long way. Pilate didn't want to be responsible for the death of an innocent man, so he symbolically washed his hands to say it wasn't his fault that Jesus would die. It was the religious leaders' fault, in his mind.

Of course, the Jewish leaders, rigidly adhering to the rules that said they couldn't put anyone to death, simply insisted that Pilate do it for them. In their eyes, they, too, were not responsible.

Pilate and the Jewish leaders were part of God's plan that Jesus would die for our sins. We see in Pilate, though, a man who knew he was doing wrong and sought to ease his conscience by blaming someone else.

The Bible says the conscience can be squelched, "They pretend to be religious, but their consciences are dead" (1 Timothy 4:2). Blaming others and refusing to take responsibility for one's actions is habit-forming, and eventually an individual may not even know he's doing wrong because his conscience is deadened by repeated sin. But Jesus, the real Savior, can help us keep our consciences working as they were designed to do.

Taking responsibility is a key step toward maturity. It also keeps our consciences alive and healthy to guide us properly. Admitting we're wrong can be scary, but it is essential if we're to face reality and break self-defeating patterns like Justin's.

What about You? What's your first thought when confronted with a mistake or wrongdoing? Think back to a time when something went wrong or someone challenged the way you had handled a situation. Did you automatically come up with reasons why you did what you did? Did you find someone else to blame? Or did you consider the fact that you might be wrong?

Take an honest look at the way you respond to difficulty and ask God to help you take responsibility when appropriate.

Take a Look Read Romans 1:18-19 and note God's response to avoidance of the truth.